Barney Butler was born in June 1926 at Maidstone in Kent. He married in March 1950 and has one daughter.

Barney was educated at Sutton Valence School and Kings College Taunton. He trained at Seale Hayne College in Devon and worked in horticulture for nine years.

In 1953 he joined the Essex Police Constabulary and served for six years, being stationed at Chelmsford and Romford.

In 1959 he started work in child care. For twelve years he worked with Barnardo's and then in Social Services Departments until he retired.

I acknowledge with gratitude the help and encouragement I have received from my wife Eileen while writing this book.

I dedicate the book to my daughter Anne, who shared many aspects of our life in Barnardo's.

GW00703446

Aunties and Uncles

Barney Butler

Pen Press

First published in Great Britain by Pen Press
an Imprint of indepenpress Publishing Ltd
25 Eastern Place
Brighton
BN2 1GJ

ISBN   978-1-906710-65-1

Printed and bound in the UK

A catalogue record of this book is available from
the British Library

Cover design Jacqueline Abromeit

CONTENTS

Part One:

The Village, Barkingside

Chapter 1

It happened on a Sunday

It happened on a Sunday. I know it was a Sunday because I read it in the Sunday newspaper. Little did I know that it was going to change our lives! It was an advertisement for house-parents for a London County Council children's home, not very far away. I lived with my wife and daughter in Harold Hill in north London. I had been in the Essex police force for nearly six years, I had passed my promotion exams and I had been told that promotion to sergeant was fairly imminent.

For a while my wife Eileen and I had been having some reservations about my job, as the shift hours I worked combined with her working hours as a teacher meant that we often saw very little of each other. Also, apart from reasons due to promotion, one had to expect to be moved to a different area every five years and we were concerned that this might have an adverse effect on Anne, our three-year-old daughter's education. We had enjoyed working together in youth clubs and had fostered a teenaged girl and we felt we had something to offer children, especially older ones.

We decided to visit this children's home and find out what the job of house-parents involved. We set off in our little Austin A30 car in a state of some anticipation wondering if we were doing the right thing or merely unsettling ourselves. When we arrived at this London County Council home, without an appointment, we were confronted by a porter at the main gate. On informing him that we wished to talk to someone about their advertisement in the Sunday newspaper we were told that he would phone the person on duty at the main house. However, when he returned he said that we would have to write away for the necessary application forms, and after these had been returned we might be offered an interview and then we could find out more about what the work entailed.

We returned home somewhat disappointed but after talking it over, we decided to take no further action for the time being. It was about four weeks later that Eileen was in the staff room at the school where she was teaching, when she happened to glance at the Times educational supplement and saw an advertisement for house-parents at Barnardo's Homes at Barkingside, Ilford, Essex, which was not very far away. We decided to drive over to Barkingside on the following Saturday afternoon and find out more. We were fortunate that the lady superintendent and her husband, the chief officer, were sitting in their garden near the main gate and the lady superintendent came over to us and asked if she could help us. Although we had visited without an appointment, and on a Saturday, we were made very welcome and we were given enough information about the work to make an appointment to visit Barkingside one evening after work and have a formal interview. We were told that this establishment was known as the village or village homes. We received very full information about what the job entailed and although the salary was very low compared to the combined salary of our present occupations we went away full of enthusiasm. We were given application forms and a promise that if we applied for the joint post of house-parents, Barnardo's would not pursue our present employers' references until they were fairly certain we would be accepted. After much thought we decided to apply for the position of house-parents and sent off the completed forms to Barnardo's.

Much to our delight, we were invited over to Barkingside one evening for a formal interview. It had to be an evening as we were not both available to go in the daytime. We were interviewed by two ladies – the lady superintendent, and a Miss Golding, who was one of four senior staff and in charge of one of four sections of the village homes. This home was built on an estate of 60 acres given by a philanthropist to Dr Barnardo when he got married. He had already started a home for boys in Stepney in London, but felt that girls needed a far more homely atmosphere. He eventually had 60 cottage homes built around three greens in the village. We were able to show we had some previous experience of children with a young daughter aged three and a half years and the involvement of fostering a teenage girl as well as helping in youth clubs. It transpired that Miss Golding was in charge of some of the main green cottages for long-stay children. That meant children who had been assessed in the reception section and were considered to need long-term care in a children's home, as opposed to being fostered. Children who were in touch with their parents usually went to a long-stay home. It soon became obvious that the ladies had already identified a position in the village that they felt would suit us both. They suggested that we might be a suitable couple to be house-parents in charge of a cottage of 12 adolescent boys aged 12 to 16 years. I think they felt an ex-teacher and an ex-policeman should be able to control 12 boys! It was suggested that we might like to go over to the cottage, and have a chat with the present house-parents.

The married couple in charge of Woodside Cottage, situated on the main green, were going to go in charge of a Barnardo's home on the south coast. They were a charming couple with two young boys. They showed us around the cottage and it was obvious that the living space for a couple in charge would be a tight fit. The cottages had originally been built to house a matron in charge and 15 to 20 girls, the senior girl acting as an assistant. Now the cottage would accommodate 12 children – in this case it would be 12 boys, a resident assistant and either a single matron in charge or as in our case a married couple in charge. There was a small room that would be my daughter's bedroom. Downstairs there was a kitchen, a utility room, children's toilet, and a playroom as well as a dining room where we all had our meals. We would have a small sitting room about 10ft square with a fireplace across one corner. We were told that as this room was such an awkward shape Barnardo's would supply a new carpet, otherwise we would supply our own furniture. This would mean we would have to part with most of our furniture and every piece we brought with us would have to fit either into our small sitting room or into our bedroom. Not only would it be a very tight fit for ourselves and our possessions, but we would have very little privacy.

After our visit, we went back to the office and were asked if we felt this would be the sort of work we had envisaged and would we be interested in applying for the joint post of house-parents in charge, subject to references from our present employers. The salary was quite low but we knew that we would be working for a charity and it was very worthwhile work. It was pointed out to us that we would get board and lodging included and Barnardo's had a non-contributory pension scheme which they financed but did not guarantee a minimum sum towards a pension. This did not worry us in the least as we felt at the time, quite wrongly, that retirement was a long way off. We agreed that we wanted to go ahead with our application and Barnardo's could take up the final references. A starting date was suggested for 1st January 1959.

We went home to await news from Barnardo's. We were in a state of limbo and time went so slowly. We started to plan for moving and deciding what we would take with us. Then we heard from Barnardo's that we had been accepted and were asked to confirm the proposed starting date. Now it was a rush to give in a month's notice to our employers. Fortunately, Eileen was in a temporary teaching post at this time, and so only one month's notice was required. We had to part with furniture that was too large or unsuitable, but also many items which we had collected during our eight years of marriage, and which had many memories for us. However, it was all in a good cause providing our change of careers to work with Barnardo's worked out all right. We finished packing and then went to spend Christmas and the remaining days of 1958 with friends.

Chapter 2

Early Days at Barkingside

It was with considerable excitement and a lot of apprehension that we drove off to Barkingside at the beginning of January 1959 to start our new areas of work. Anne was wedged in the back seat of the car, grasping tightly on to 'Tigger', her favourite stuffed toy, surrounded by bags of last-minute items. We had another ten days of living out of suitcases before we would be united with our furniture and the rest of our belongings. We were going to stay in the staff accommodation in Mossford Lodge in the Barnardo's village for the first ten days while Mary and John, the couple in charge of Woodside, showed us the ropes. After ten days Mary and John would move down to the south coast and take over a Barnardo's home there, and we would then be responsible for Woodside.

We were soon introduced to the 12 boys who were living in the cottage. There was Tony who was 16 years old, and held the position of head prefect for the village; Peter was aged 15 years; Fred, Chris, Richard and Henry were all 14-year-olds. The younger group included four 12-year-olds, namely Arthur, in his first year at grammar school, Dennis, Michael and Stephen; also, Eric who was aged 11, and ten-year-old Frank (the brother of Stephen).

Eileen was instructed in various duties. These included getting familiar with the daily cottage routines for meals, bedtimes etc, as well as medical matters, laundry and domestic arrangements. The main adjustment was coming to terms with the quantities of food required for 15 people! Although a good cook Eileen does not rate cooking as one of her favourite activities, so it was going to be a very different life for Eileen compared to her teaching days!

John gave me a guided tour of the village, and we started at the main green, which was used for all the outdoor sports, namely football, cricket and athletics. The remains of the markings on the grass for the various activities held last year were still just visible. We walked across the green from our cottage to the Wendy hut where all the sports equipment was stored and where it seemed I would be spending quite a lot of time. The hut was quite small and was dominated by rows and rows of football boots. On our way, round John frequently stopped and introduced me to various members of the staff who worked in the village. I wondered if I would ever remember all their names. I felt very much like a new boy at school. Leaving the Wendy hut we passed the hospital where children, and in some cases staff, could be admitted if they became seriously unwell. The children had their six-monthly medical check-up and eyesight test here and the hospital also catered for long-term hospitalised children.

Beyond the hospital, we came to another 'green', but this was really just a grass field on which were two buildings, the swimming pool and the nursery school. We went over and examined the swimming pool, which was empty. It was quite large and was in the open air with wooden changing rooms down each side. I was told that it did not have a filtration plant and had to be emptied and the algae scrubbed off two or three times during the summer, and I would be involved in these procedures. The nursery school catered for the pre-school age children living in the village as well as those of staff members. I would soon become familiar with this building as it had been agreed Anne could attend the nursery.

We moved on, passing a hall where entertainment or meetings were held, and I was told that visiting groups of Barnardo's supporters were entertained with a cup of tea here after they had been given a tour of the village. John said it was probable that I would be involved in conducting some of these tours. We then visited the clothing store where new children were given any clothing they needed. The store was presided over by a delightful lady, who unfortunately suffered from a severely disfigured face due to a fire accident in childhood and had herself been cared for by Barnardo's. Nearby was Mossford School, which was used by the children in the reception unit who were only in the village for a short while, as this was less disrupting for them and for the schools in the locality.

We continued our journey round the village and came to the church, which was brick built and large enough to seat all the children and staff. The village chaplain, the Rev James Brown, a Methodist minister held a morning and evening service on a Sunday and our boys would be expected to attend both services. We went inside and I was shown the two pews that were allocated to the staff and boys of our cottage. On leaving the church, we then found ourselves on the nursery green. The cottages around this green were home to babies and very young children, and were staffed by trained nursery nurses. We then made our way to the reception green. The cottages here housed children who were new admissions to the village. We turned into a road running between reception green and the rear of some cottages on main green, including Woodside.

Back at Woodside, we were joined by Mary and Eileen and the four of us sat down and chatted about the village. The cottages were run by a single lady or a married couple, with one or two assistants. The lady in charge was called Matron, a title, I would guess, dating back to pre-war days. In the case of a married couple, the husband would usually be out at work, and the wife would run the cottage. Quite a few of the men were teachers, and got their board and lodging free in return for helping in the cottage during the evenings, weekends and school holidays. I was taking over John's position as one of the two house-fathers in the long-stay unit on the main green who were in full-time employment with Barnardo's, and was taking over some of the jobs that he normally did. These included issuing out football boots and re-studding them ready for the Saturday morning games, which all the fit boys were expected to attend. I also had to make sure there were sufficient footballs for the games. These were leather footballs that had to be cleaned, and have dubbin rubbed into the leather. They had a rubber bladder inside which had to be pumped up and then the ball had to be laced up – a time consuming occupation compared to using modern plastic balls today.

During the next few weeks, I was asked to take over on Tuesday evenings, a physical exercise (PE) class, which the officer in charge had been running. Not being a schoolteacher I really thought that this was a 'no go' area for me. However, I was given a booklet on the subject and I promised to do my best. I was also told that I would be responsible for taking parties of interested visitors around the village on Thursdays when necessary. The cottages on the main green took it in turn to be 'open' on such visiting days when everything would be given an extra shine.

The first ten days were probably the quietest time we ever had in Barnardo's, with little responsibility, but very hard work. We had just ten days to get to know the boys and form some relationship with them. We had the general running of the cottage to cope with and I was being given some tasks outside of the cottage routine.

Chapter 3

Baptism by Fire

It was now a case of 'all hands to the pumps' except we did not have any extra hands! We were told that owing to a shortage of staff, we would not be able to have an assistant house-mother for a few weeks. So, ten days after our start, we found ourselves alone with 12 boys in the cottage. It was still the school holidays. Eileen had the dinner to cook, I had the children to amuse, and together we had to supervise the arrival of our furniture. Then there was a knock at the front door. Eileen went to the door and there stood a little girl who said she wanted to speak to the matron. Eileen was not used to being called the matron and suggested that she tried the hospital. The poor girl must have been confused, as much as we were during those early days!

The boys had called our predecessors by their surname prefixed by 'Uncle' or 'Auntie'. Thus, we became 'Auntie Butler' and 'Uncle Butler'. We were surprised to learn that only one of the boys was an orphan; in fact, he was the only orphan we had in our care in our 12 years with Barnardo's. Most of the children were in care because their own parent or parents were unable to look after them, for various reasons. Some of the children were placed by a local authority, usually because they were in need of long-term care. We had one boy in the cottage who was placed there because he was on probation for two years and it was a condition of the probation order that he should live away from his home for this time, but he was allowed to go home for weekends.

We had completed our first day's work on our own; our furniture had arrived and we had managed to get our beds up and now Anne was settled in reasonable comfort in her room. So far, Anne was taking the change very well and enjoying the large family, but the boys were not so keen on having a girl in their cottage. We were very tired as we got into bed that night, but we reviewed the day's events and surmised that it had gone quite well. Our thoughts were very much concerned with the present, but we did wonder what the future held, and we just hoped we had done the right thing in giving up our jobs and the privacy of our own home. Time would tell!

The boys were used to a fairly regimental regime and saw this as a time to test the boundaries and see how far they could go, having as much fun as they could. In their defence, it could be argued that they too felt confused and unsettled by yet another change in their lives. It was a question of not making sudden changes and giving the boys respect if we wanted their respect. We knew the boys would not have any respect if they thought we were a 'soft touch'. The difficulty was that the boys knew the rules better than we did ourselves.

Just outside of the back entrance to the village was a nightclub called the Ranch House Club. In front of the building was a western style full size four-wheel carriage on a permanent mount. On a rare – in those early days – visit to the shops, I saw Eric and another boy playing on the carriage. I proceeded to tell Eric that he should come down from the carriage, but Eric insisted that he had permission from the owners to play on the carriage. Later that day I spoke to Tony, the senior boy. I asked him if Eric had indeed permission from the owners to play on the carriage. With a wry smile he said, no, he hadn't got permission. Tony would never grass on his peers in the cottage but would give an honest answer when questioned. Lesson number one was assimilated; if in doubt ask Tony!

We soon had support from our executive officer, Miss Golding, who answered many of our questions. We were told at our original interview that we were entitled to three weeks' holiday a year, two-

and-a-half days off every two months and a day off each week. We would find later on that we could take two hours off in the afternoons when the children were at school. Miss Golding said that as we did not have an assistant we could not take any time off except during school hours, but she pointed out that she would try and get a relief house-mother in order to give us a day off. From our own point of view, it would be best to get on top of the job before taking much time off, so we were not too worried but looked forward to having an assistant house-mother.

I had to go over to Mossford School hall to take my first PE class, a task that, for sure, was not going to be one of my favourites! The deputy chief officer (whom I will refer to as the deputy) met me in good time and explained that I was expected to occupy the boys for an hour! Soon the boys started to arrive, and it seemed that all the boys in the village had arrived, but it in fact it was no more than 25 to 30 boys aged between ten and 14 years old. These PE classes were compulsory for all the older boys in the village. The deputy started off by lining the boys up in three rows and very soon had them running on the spot and put them through numerous exercises that were in the book I had been given to read. I then was given the daunting task of taking over while the deputy looked on. I was beginning to wish I had never applied for this job. Eileen and I were tired from the continuous work without time off. The deputy eventually left me to my own devices, having checked that the boys were not running wild but in some sense of order. How glad I was when the hour was up and I could go home.

Although we had some experience of children, we soon found the difference when we had them for 24 hours a day! Fortunately, I enjoyed table games and hobbies such as model making and stamp collecting. Children respond readily to a stimulus and a new activity can become a craze, which I soon discovered, and provided one brought the activity to a finish before they got bored with it, the activity could be repeated again in the future. If it was a continuous activity, such as stamp collecting, then it was little and often.

When we took over the cottage, the boys were busy playing pontoon for matchsticks and were getting quite bored with it. I suggested that they played a more difficult game such as Bridge. I taught them a very simple way of evaluating their hand and what was needed in points to open the bidding or respond or no bid. I was surprised how quickly they took up the challenge and learned to play. I think they were bored at the end of the Christmas holidays and were pleased to have the attention of a fresh adult. It was very satisfying to hear them come into meals discussing their hands and their bidding.

The boys had their different bedtimes according to age and although they were not supposed to talk after lights out, there was the occasional whisper. However, I drew the line when I found one 12-year-old had three lighted birthday candles under the sheets in his bed! It was a case of "See you in my study after breakfast".

I found that I was gradually able to get the boys interested in various activities that they enjoyed, some of which were testing such as cycling and camping. They wanted to please me rather than miss out. In other words, I was giving them the opportunity to have legal excitement instead of getting into trouble through boredom. But I still had to have a punishment for the wrong doers and I devised a plan. I would call the delinquent into my sitting room (I did not have the luxury of a study or office) and I would give him a good 'talking to'. Being half Irish, I suppose the gift of the gab helped. These sessions became known among the boys as 'Uncle's penny lectures', and they hated them! It certainly sufficed as a controlling punishment most of the time. For really bad behaviour, I would have to resort to barring them from some activity. Of course, the punishment must fit the crime and boys will usually accept a punishment if they feel it is fair.

As we came to the end of the first week, Eileen was told to go out and purchase two nylon overalls to wear in the cottage and Barnardo's would pay the cost back to her. Eileen hated those overalls! On Sunday we had to make sure the boys were in their Sunday suits, hair brushed and combed and off we went to the village church. All eyes were on us, especially those of the hierarchy, to see if and how we controlled the boys. The older boys sat behind and Eileen. Anne and I sat in the middle of the front pew, with the younger boys on each side of us. I heard a whispered chuckle behind me and I reached round behind myself and scooped up a book. 'The powers that be' were apparently quite impressed and I soon had a reputation for having eyes in the back of my head. The boys were expected to attend church again in the evening. We were expected to have Bible reading and prayers each morning before breakfast, the boys taking it in turn to read from the Bible.

After we had been in the village for six weeks Miss Golding told us that she had arranged for a relief house-mother to come and give us a day off. We would be off duty from when the boys left for school until early evening. Although it was not exactly a whole day off it was a very welcome break for us. Unfortunately, the day off was to be Tuesday when I had the PE class and I was advised by Miss Golding to see if the deputy could arrange for someone else to take my class. I managed to find the deputy and made this request as I was taking a day off, my first one for six weeks. He gave me a stinging reply, asking me why I thought I needed a day off. He then said that he did not have a day off for two months when he first came to the village. However, he finally agreed to find a replacement.

We looked forward a great deal to our day off. It was like being let out of school. It was the week before our ninth wedding anniversary and we planned to make the most of it. We would take Anne out of nursery school for the day, do a little shopping, and then visit our friends who were not too far away. The relief house-mother duly arrived about nine- thirty. She was a retired member of the Barnardo's staff, and having handed over to her, we set off in our car with Anne in the back seat happily taking everything in her stride. First stop was to do some shopping, buying some essentials and enjoying a cup of coffee. Next stop was to visit a large store to buy a few items to make our sitting room a little more comfortable. Having completed our shopping we had our lunch in the restaurant. Eileen enjoyed the first meal that she hadn't cooked for six weeks! We then went off to visit our friends with whom we had stayed for Christmas, which seemed a long time ago. Our friends were very interested to know how we had been getting on. Life felt very different, talking about our new jobs and relaxing with a cup of tea. Soon it was time to return to reality and go back to what was now our home. We returned in time for Anne's bedtime, and although the boys seemed rather lively, the house-mother said everything was all right and she bade us goodnight.

Next morning we had a visit from Miss Golding and she was not very pleased. She said that the boys had been out of control while we were out. She described the scene as she went past the cottage; the front door was flung open and one of the boys' coats was thrown out onto the ground. When she went into the cottage to investigate, she found one of the younger boys was locked in the bicycle shed. After giving us a strong lecture, she swept out of the cottage. Eileen and I discussed the matter and decided that it was not our fault how the boys behaved in our absence, as after all we'd only had a little time to make relationships with them. We felt that it was Barnardo's responsibility to provide a suitable relief, especially as there was not an assistant house-mother to help the relief person. Eileen and I went straight down to the office and demanded to see Miss Golding. We stated our case and said if Barnardo's could not support us with suitable staff we would have to leave their employment as it was obvious we could not run the cottage without help and some time off. We did not really want to leave and Miss Golding's attitude changed from that day and she gave us more support and respect. She was a lady of the old school and even long-established house-mothers would be wary of taking their full leave entitlement. We were to have a good relationship with Miss Golding in the future.

Little did we know that we had one more hurdle to get over that month. Two weeks later we both went down with 'flu. We were told by the doctor to take to our bed while our temperatures were up. They had to provide temporary help in the cottage while we were laid low. The village chaplain, James Browne, took the boys for walks and later told us that Fred had behaved so badly that he would never take him out for organised activities. Fred was later to do well at work and we have been in touch with each other ever since.

One day as we recuperated the relief house-mother decided to tempt us with rice pudding. We thought we were more ill than we had believed as we could not eat the rice pudding – it transpired that one of the boys had put salt in the sugar container! We decided that it was time we got up and made our presence felt.

Chapter 4

Settling In

Good news! Miss Golding had just visited us and said that they had interviewed a young lady who could be a suitable assistant house-mother for our cottage, and that she would bring her round to see us after lunch. This was indeed exciting news, especially for Eileen, as she had to bear the brunt of the staff shortage. Eileen hoped she liked cooking! In due course Joan was brought to the cottage and Miss Golding left us together so that we could show Joan round and explain what the work would entail.

Joan was a very pleasant young lady who had a younger brother and sister whom she was used to looking after. She appeared to quite accept the domestic chores and yes, she liked cooking! We showed her the rather small bedroom, which would be her refuge when off duty, and then took her round the cottage. Over a cup of tea in our sitting room, we briefly described the boys who lived with us. We talked about the routine we were trying to establish. But, as we told Joan, we were still finding our way with such a large family, as we had only been at Woodside for two months. However, Joan indicated that she would like to come and work in our cottage, and would be able to start in two weeks' time. Miss Golding seemed pleased that Joan wanted to come and confirmed that she could start work when she had suggested.

We now had to establish some routine in the cottage, as much to give the boys a feeling of security as to make life easier for ourselves as well as for Joan.

I had been asked to take responsibility for photographing all the new children when they were first admitted to the village. These photographs were to be kept on the case files, to be a reminder of the child to all present when the social worker held a case conference. Such was the backlog that I needed to take 50 photographs a week. First of all I had to sort out the lighting problem. In the 50s, one usually relied on disposable flash bulbs but this was going to cost me a fortune, so a visit to the local photographic shop was suggested. I was shown the latest device, an electronic flash gun. This had to be charged up by plugging it into the mains and would give 50 to 60 flashes on a single charge. It was quite bulky, heavy and expensive but it solved my problem. I don't think I ever got my money back on this investment! I agreed to take photographs on Tuesday mornings, and then, when I had the prints back from the shop, I would show the house-mother the photos and I would get more printed for them if they wished.

The Easter holidays were approaching and one of the highlights was the annual cross-country race, which gave an excuse for the boys to get covered in mud. For the purpose of stimulating interest in sporting events, the cottages were divided into Red team and Blue team. Woodside was in the Blue team. I was asked to be responsible for organising Blue team. There were just two races, one for boys of 14 and over and one for the under 14s. The races were run in Hainault Forest about three or four miles away. This is an open forest, with just the odd tree but plenty of undulating ground that made the races interesting. Once the clocks were put forward, the boys were able to practise, by running round the main green after school for three or four laps. Anne thought this was great fun and toddled after the boys for as long as she could. The course was carefully marked out each year by members of staff who knew the course by heart. On the day, the weather was wet and windy and the ground was very muddy. Our only success that year was that Tony managed to win the senior's race. Many of the house-mothers turned up to watch and encourage their boys. Some of the female staff sensibly turned up in trousers. A few days later, a note went round from the chief officer saying that while trousers were, in the circumstances, appropriate clothing for house-mothers attending the cross-country races, it was hoped that they would not be worn in the cottages. I think fashions were slow to penetrate the bastions of Barnardo's in those days!

When we arrived at Woodside, we brought our own television set with us. We found that Barnardo's did not supply televisions to the cottages but left it to the cottage staff to let the children watch their own television. We felt that it was good for the children to see some television, mainly because it was now part of life. Most families had television and it made our children even more conspicuous if they were not familiar with some of the current programmes. As our set had only a 9-in screen and could not receive the commercial programme called ITV, we decided to rent a 12-in screen model, which could receive ITV. We had it installed in the playroom, as it was not practical to have 12 boys in our sitting room to watch television. You can imagine that our popularity went up a notch or two.

Another annual event was the inter-cottage hobbies competition in which each cottage could display the results of their children's hobbies. I noticed that cooking featured largely with the girls who also displayed some nice needlework. Unfortunately we did not have anything to enter, however I vowed to have some hobbies for the boys to enter the next year.

I was pleased to note that the PE class closed for the summer term and holidays. I knew that the boys did not enjoy the class and I felt the same way. Children in their own homes were not forced to do PE once a week. I knew it helped to keep the lads occupied but I felt surely there were more pleasant ways of doing that. I had decided one evening to try something more interesting and after putting the boys through a few exercises, I organised a game of football in the gym. As numbers were too great to have them all playing at once, I divided the boys into three teams, the team sitting out were to play the winners. After 20 minutes, we had a winning team who duly took on those sitting out, and the losers were now spectators. We had just started a new game, and the boys were thoroughly enjoying themselves, when who should walk in but the deputy. He demanded to know why the boys were sitting out and why was I not making them do their exercises. The deputy then lined the boys up in rows and gave them their exercises. He then told me that I was not to let them play football again. The way he handled the situation completely undermined my authority and also my confidence. I decided that before the winter came I would think of some alternative activities.

The beginning of the summer term meant the filling up of the swimming pool. This would take at least two days and one got frequent bulletins from the children on its progress. Once it was in use, we could take the boys along two or even three times a day at weekends. Needless to say, most of the boys could swim quite well and it was a very happy way for them to use up their energies, especially on a hot summer's day. I did not have any responsibility for the running of the pool, except when the water would go a trifle green in colour. The pool would then be drained, which took almost as long as it took to fill. When empty it was a case of all available male staff being expected to help to remove the algae with a scrubbing brush dipped in chlorine. It was a most unpleasant job and had to be done several times a season.

Chapter 5

Summer Days

The children went back to school for the summer term, the weather became warmer and we began to establish a summer routine in the cottage. The older boys in the village were expected to take part in a game of cricket on the main green once a week and the men were to take turns umpiring these games. The chief officer was particularly interested in cricket and took charge of the first team, coaching the boys and arranging fixtures, which were against school teams and took place on a Saturday. Sometimes we had a picnic tea on the green outside our cottage and watched the cricket match. Once a week I found myself umpiring one of the minor games on a distant corner of the green.

I was asked if I would organise the athletics for the village, including sports days. The sports arrangements included a village sports day with the track events being contested by Blue and Red teams. The winning children would be selected for the area finals, which would be held at another Barnardo's home. The winners at the area finals would then go forward to the inter-homes sport's day, which was to be held in the village, when many other staff and children would be present. This event held an important place on the Barnardo's calendar. I would be responsible for the running of this event, but fortunately, I would previously have had the experience of the village sports day. Having agreed to this responsibility, I was then presented with a starting pistol – as a token of office?

Preparing the track turned out to be more complicated than it sounded. Firstly, I had to mark out the track, of which I could see faint traces, as it had been marked out the previous year in creosote. As the green was too small for a track of four laps to the mile, it had to be marked up to allow five laps to the mile. This also affected the measurement of the staggered starts. I managed to trace a sufficient amount of the old creosote lines to mark out the running track in creosote. These lines would be gone over with whiting before the actual sports events. Meanwhile I checked out some of the equipment for the hurdles. They consisted of two uprights joined at the base. The uprights had small holes drilled into them and a small wooden dowel was inserted in order to adjust the height. A bamboo cane was laid across the top of the dowels which would fall off fairly painlessly when struck by the athlete. These bamboo canes were painted alternate bands of black and white. When I went to repaint the black part, with the help of Chris one evening, I couldn't open the paint tin. Whilst looking for a more suitable screwdriver, Chris managed to open the tin, but splashed the paint over my new white shirt! Never turn your back...! Another lesson to assimilate. On the whole, the boys were quite keen to help with such tasks and it was a natural opportunity to gain a one-to-one relationship with a boy.

As sports day loomed nearer, I had to think about forming a Blue team. We used to practise after school and I well remember one slightly damp evening, two 12-year-olds arriving from a cottage for practice in the hurdles event, wearing blue gabardine macs over their running shorts and shirts. When I suggested that they would find it easier jumping over the hurdles without their macs they said that they had strict instructions not to take off their macs in case they caught a cold in the damp air!

The day before sports day, I decided that it would be wise to make sure that the starting pistol was working all right. On one side of our cottage we had a girls' cottage and on the side of our bedroom, the neighbouring cottage was used as a child guidance clinic. As I kept the pistol in our bedroom for security, it was only natural to fire the pistol out of the window. It went off with such a loud bang and after a fraction of a second's silence, all the sash windows on that side of the child guidance clinic seemed to open simultaneously, and heads popped out with looks of amazement or horror. When I explained that I was testing a starting pistol, I got a lot of unbelieving looks. I think they were convinced I had shot my wife!

Hoping for dry weather, I marked out the lines of the track in white. Good weather prevailed and we had a successful sports day, and what was more the Blue team won by a narrow margin – and no, the two boys did not have to hurdle in their macs!

The next stage was to make sure, if possible, the winners were able to run in the area finals, which in our case would be held at Goldings Technical Training School. This was a Barnardo's home situated in Hertfordshire, for boys aged 14 years who wanted to learn a trade. They had a choice of shoemaking, gardening, decorating, carpentry or printing. In the latter case, they would complete a full five-year apprenticeship.

We fortunately had several winners at the area finals, who were automatically selected to appear in the inter-homes sports, which would take place in July. The grass on the main green was specially cut for the big day and I went round the track with my white line marker. The weather was kind to us and everything went off all right, much to my relief. I must admit my attention was more directed to keeping everything under control than in supporting the team from the village. I had to leave the supporting role to other members of staff.

The summer holidays had now started and our next test would be to see how we coped with keeping the boys occupied during the long break from school. We found that frequent trips to the swimming pool helped both to occupy the boys as well as a chance for them to use up their energy, and it was a very popular activity. The cottages with younger children would go to the seaside for a week or two, each cottage organising their own holiday. They would hire a church hall for the holiday and a Barnardo's van would take their equipment as well as an old but serviceable mattress for each person to sleep on. However, the older boys in the village went to the big annual

Barnardo's camp at West Runton, near Sherringham on the Norfolk coast and this included all our family. Consequently, we were informed that we would be closing our cottage for two weeks and Eileen, our assistant Auntie Joan, and I would accompany them for the first two weeks. The camp went on for a further two weeks but it would then have a complete change of staff and boys. The chief officer and his wife would be in charge for the first two weeks. The boys lost no time in telling us all about the camp and tales, imaginary or otherwise, of previous camps.

The day for departure arrived and the boys and Auntie Joan travelled up to West Runton by coach. We loaded up our car with our clothes, and bits and pieces that we thought might make camp life more comfortable, and then with Anne settled comfortably in the back seat among our possessions, we set off into the unknown! It was quite a long journey for our small car, which was bursting at the seams with the load. When we at long last arrived, we found that the camp had been set up and all the boys had arrived safely along with Joan and other staff. There were about 40 boys in the camp, most of whom were from the village but also there were a few boys who were fostered and came to the camp to give the foster parents a break.

The boys slept on straw palliasses in four man ridge tents, which were pitched meticulously in two straight lines in the centre of the camp. Beyond these tents was the staff accommodation in larger ex-army ridge tents. Staff had the use of some old narrow iron beds, which offered a degree of comfort. A large marquee was used as the dining tent for everyone, while a smaller marquee was used as the food store. Cooking was done in a portable wooden shed and food preparation and washing-up was done in the open whenever possible. Toilet facilities and ablutions were equally primitive but we did have access to an oval galvanised bathtub, in which Anne could have a bath. At least the boys got a daily bath in the sea!

We soon got into the time honoured routine of camp life. The boys were roused at 7am, had their wash and then breakfast. Each of the boys' tents took it in turn to wash up for the day, helped of course by the staff. The next hour was fully occupied for the boys, who were preparing for the daily tent inspection. Including the officer in charge there were two other men from the village as well as myself and we took it in turns to inspect the tents. Each tent had a boy nominated as leader and he would be responsible for the state of his tent. His task was made easier as cash prizes of one shilling and sixpence for each boy in the best tent, one shilling each for the runners-up and sixpence each for the third placed tent were offered. This addition to their pocket money was a real incentive and they would spend the time lining up their kit with spare clothes neatly folded on their blankets and toothbrush, toothpaste, brush and comb lined up on top to the nearest eighth of an inch. The sides of the tents were neatly rolled up and the boys even brushed the grass both inside and in front of the tents. I did not look forward to my first inspection, as it appeared to me that all the tents looked equally immaculate. I watched closely as the other men did their inspections. It would not do to award all this money to the wrong tents, as it was, after all, a serious business for the boys.

Tent inspection over, it was time for the daily swim in the sea just below the campsite. The site was very large and was occupied by both individual families and organisations. The beach was approached by a tricky scramble down some cliffs, which fortunately were not very high. There was a warning sign to take care but unfortunately, one boy thought he would find a different route to the top, and broke his arm. This was the only serious injury we had during the fortnight. Once on the beach we erected two flagpoles to mark the extent of the bathing area and we all had a splash if not a swim. The swim was followed by a game of football when the flagpoles enjoyed a new role as goal posts.

After the football we returned to the camp where everyone seemed be ready for their dinner. When the washing-up was completed, pocket money was distributed and the boys headed into the nearby town of Sheringham, which was about 30 minutes' walk away. This gave all the staff a valuable break and time to make preparations for any other activities. I was feeling quite shattered by now.

The boys were quite punctual at returning because the next item on the agenda was high tea, which consisted of something savoury, and bread and butter with spreads and cake. With all this fresh air, I had gained a healthy appetite and so had Eileen and Anne. I found that after a day or two Anne seemed to be fully integrated in the activities of the camp and was accepted by the boys and indeed made friends with the younger ones. It helped that she was willing to join in all the activities to the best of her ability and with great enthusiasm.

Teatime was followed by the usual washing-up and then we played a great favourite game with the children, called Puttocks. It was a form of Tip and Run cricket and had the advantage that any number could play and play was continuous. There were two stumps each end, about 15yds apart, the stumps being placed as in cricket but with the middle one missing. The ball, usually a tennis ball, was bowled from either end, underarm, without waiting for the batsman to take his place! A new batsman coming in could be bowled out before he even reached the crease if he wasn't very quick taking his place. The bat was sometimes a baseball bat; otherwise a cricket bat was used. The batsman could be bowled out if the ball hit the stumps and half out if it went between them. Everyone joined in, including the staff, and because it was played non-stop, everyone had an innings, even if there were 15 to 20 players a side. I wasn't very good at hitting the ball but I could run quite fast so I didn't let my side down too badly. Unfortunately Anne was a little too young and it was her bedtime so she didn't play, but Eileen was able to bat quite well as she was used to rounders.

On one or two occasions, the chief officer would set a quiz based on local knowledge, particularly of Sheringham, which kept the lads occupied for the afternoon. These quizzes were very popular with the boys as there were monetary prizes for the top three teams.

One evening when all the children were settled down, I had a stroll along the top of the cliffs with the chief officer and he enquired how I felt I was getting along. I talked about my PE class and my misgivings and I suggested that I ran a Badminton class on that evening, lasting one hour for up to eight boys and one hour for up to eight girls. I said there was room in the school hall if I could have permission to paint the necessary lines. I said I would endeavour to buy some second-hand racquets. To my delight, the chief officer readily agreed. After all, he was getting two hours work from me instead of one hour. I looked forward to getting the badminton class under way. The problem would be to get enough girls wanting to come. I could make sure I got enough boys from my cottage alone, although I would have preferred volunteers!

The two weeks passed quite quickly, but I think most of the staff, including Eileen and I, were looking forward to 'home comforts' when we returned to Barkingside. The boys had enjoyed a break from routine and it had broken up the long summer holiday but I think they were happy to go home, but not so keen at the thought of going back to school. And so, once again, our little car was loaded to the roof and we said goodbye to West Runton and Norfolk. The tents were all left erected for there was a fresh party of boys and staff coming for the next two weeks. We nearly did not leave Norfolk, for a big end on the engine of our car started to make expensive noises, and so I had to drive slowly home wondering if we would make it or whether we would come to a shuddering halt on the way. We did make it home but I found that I had to have a reconditioned engine fitted, which was an expense we could have done without.

It was after seven o'clock in the evening when we eventually rolled up outside Woodside Cottage. Joan and the boys had arrived home in time for a late lunch, but Joan was puzzled as to what had become of us, and was wondering how she would cope on her own. The boys, on the contrary, were, I would guess, a little less worried!

Chapter 6

Autumn

We soon settled back into our usual routine and I felt the boys were glad to be back in familiar surroundings. Anne seemed very happy to return to her home. It was very important to get her settled again, after so much change that year. While the boys were making the most of the two weeks remaining before school started, now was the time for me to get some jobs done.

Firstly, there were the badminton court lines to be painted before the school hall was in use again. I then had to acquire at least four badminton rackets and my first resource to check would entail a visit to Stepney Causeway, headquarters of Barnardo's. At headquarters they had a 'Gift-in-Kind' department where all the non-monetary gifts were stored. Staff could come up to Stepney and choose suitable items for their 'home'. It was a source of games for the boys to play, as well as books and items useful for the cottage. To my delight, I found three badminton rackets in reasonable condition with their wooden presses. As Eileen and I both had rackets ourselves, we could supplement the other three for the time being. Shuttlecocks I would have to buy. Next, I needed a net and I would have to make up some posts, and time was running out. At least I did not have to worry about the deputy chief officer and his PE classes.

Tony and Peter were school leavers and Peter had returned to his extended family as a working boy. Tony's social worker had found him an office job in City Road, London. Tony would have very little money left after he had paid for his lodgings, but it was a starting point for him. He was eventually to get a job in the Civil Service.

Boys and girls who had left school were invited to headquarters in batches of eight or ten youngsters to a leavers' farewell ceremony. I accompanied Tony for my first experience of the ceremony and very nearly got farewelled myself! When I arrived I was directed with Tony to a small room where other boys were waiting and as I neither knew anyone at headquarters nor knew my way round, I waited patiently with the boys who were there to be farewelled. Eventually, a man came and asked for our names. He found he had one too many boys! When I explained who I was, he apologised and said he thought I was one of the boys to be farewelled! I must have looked young in those days although I was over 30 years of age. In due course, Tony was fitted out with a suit, and given a Bible and a fountain pen. The latter was given with the address of the chairman of the Management Committee and Tony was told that he was expected to write to the chairman after he had been at work a few months to tell him how he was getting on. By now, I was getting hungry and was glad to find that lunch was the next item on the agenda. I went along to the canteen with the other boys as well as Tony. After an enjoyable meal, we all went into the chapel for a short service and then it was time to return to Barkingside.

It was now time to get the boys ready for their return to school. We had one boy, Arthur, attending grammar school, and the rest of the boys were divided between three secondary schools in Barkingside and Ilford, except for Frank who was still of junior school age and went to Mossford School in the village. For Eric it was a case of changing schools to go up to a senior school and he was quite anxious about it. Eric enjoyed the attention he got when he went shopping for his school uniform with Eileen. Barnardo's policy with school uniform, which was an expensive item, was that it was important for the children not to appear different to the other pupils at the school, as they already were not living with their own family. Arthur was the only boy who seemed to have serious home-work now that Tony had left school, and we had to make sure he had a quiet spot for his studies. The boys went back to school, looking very neat and tidy in their school uniforms, at the beginning of the new term. We were enjoying some lovely summer weather and back in the cottage the staff relaxed for the first time since the school holidays had begun.

On our day off after the boys went back to school, we decided to buy a portable stereo record player when we saw quite an inexpensive one in the shops. We felt that, at this time, we could not afford to buy more than one record to play on it and we chose the musical show *South Pacific.* We were relaxing after lunch one school day, and were playing this record when Eileen went into our backyard to bring in some tea towels from the clothes line. Eileen was singing along with the record when she came to the words "and ain't it too damn bad" just as the chaplain turned the corner into our backyard! He looked a bit puzzled at Eileen's language until we explained the circumstances. He said he had not heard of stereo records, or the show.

James, the chaplain, then explained the reason for his visit. He said he had been asked to form a club for the older children, aged 13 years and upwards, and it would be focussed on preparing children to work for the Duke of Edinburgh Award. He asked me if I would assist him in this scheme and I said I would of course be very pleased to help. The plan was to gather together some suitable bicycles and teach the boys map reading and then teach them camping skills in the spring. The girls would be integrated into the scheme later but we would start with the boys. In the meantime, he asked if Eileen would take a group of girls for netball on Saturday mornings, as a start. We would soon be needing two assistant house-mothers to keep the cottage going while we undertook these extra activities! We did not really mind – I think we both liked to be busy and felt we were doing something useful with the children.

During the autumn, the chaplain got the local police to run a cycling proficiency course for the older children, a pass being necessary before they were allowed on the public roads. All of the older boys in our cottage were successful and that meant I could take them out for some cycle rides on the roads and build up their confidence. Our highlight was a ride to Chelmsford in the spring when we took sandwiches for our lunch and ate them in the park at Chelmsford. The boys were so full of themselves after their achievement; you would have thought they had just explored darkest Africa. After a good rest to relieve aching muscles we returned home, but not before we had one alarming incident. One moment I was cycling with five boys along a country road with not a car in sight and the next moment I could see only four boys. My heart did a leap as I took in the situation, when out of the rather deep ditch bordering the road emerged the ginger-coloured head of Henry, who was quite unharmed by his experience and fortunately, neither was his bicycle! Apparently, Henry had turned his head round to talk to the boy behind and steered into the deep grass-covered ditch. After that little lesson we all returned home safely, having covered some 45 miles and with very good appetites for our tea. The boys were really proud of their achievement. It was important that their self-confidence was improved as they mixed with people at school and socially, before going out to work.

As the evenings drew in, I thought now was the time to start some indoor hobbies. As a former keen stamp collector, I was delighted to see that one or two of the boys collected stamps in a general way. I encouraged them to collect a theme, such as animals or flowers, rather than collect any stamp; also to arrange them neatly in loose-leaf albums, and write up the date of issue and other interesting details. Once again, the 'Gifts in Kind' department came to our aid. Other boys also started to take an interest in stamp collecting.

One day we were talking about model aeroplanes and the boys mentioned that the local people flew model aeroplanes on Wanstead flats on a Sunday afternoon. Richard and Dennis took up my offer to drive over and watch the planes flying. Arthur and Chris decided to come along for the ride. And so we set off to begin what turned out to be an enduring hobby of aero-modelling for countless children in our care. Model planes had been one of my boyhood interests so

I felt quite confident of encouraging the boys in our cottage to take up the hobby. As I hoped, the boys started asking questions regarding the cost and the difficulties. When we got home, we had a discussion and I said I would prove it was not a difficult hobby. I would make a small plane of balsa wood with about a 10-in wingspan, which would take off from the ground on its own elastic band power. I went into Barkingside on the following Monday afternoon and to my delight, I found a friendly model shop. I purchased a pair of small wheels, some piano wire for the undercarriage and propeller shaft and a propeller. I also had to buy some balsa wood and some glue. Little did the proprietor know what a good customer I would soon become.

I made my little aeroplane on a free evening that week in front of an interested audience. To my relief the plane became airborne off the playroom floor at the second attempt. The boys were quite impressed and wanted to make one for themselves, which meant another visit to the model shop. We planned a trip together to the shop on the following Saturday, when we bought the materials for them to make a small plane for themselves, similar to the one I had demonstrated. The boys started to ask how much it would cost to build a large one like the ones they saw at Wanstead flats. When they saw the price of the kits they realised that they would have to start saving their pocket money if they wanted to build a big model plane. We made another visit to Wanstead flats and now nearly everyone wanted to build a plane.

We now had a problem. As the boys managed to save up and buy a model kit, we had a problem of finding enough space for them to build their models and then store the partly-built models when not being worked on. Richard, Henry, Arthur, Dennis and Stephen all managed to afford to purchase a kit each, and they had to share tables. On one occasion, Chris threatened to put another boy's head through the window if he jogged his arm again, and promptly demonstrated what he had threatened to do, and broke the window. Fortunately, the other boy did not suffer even a scratch from the incident, but I had a bit of explaining to do to my boss. Chris had to suffer one of my 'penny lectures' when I told him that while I accepted that it was an accident it was a dangerous way to behave and could have resulted in a serious injury to the other boy. I told him that if this happened again he would have to contribute to the cost of repairs. One thing, it showed that the boys were taking a pride in their work, and I thought to myself, long may it last. One boy, Charlie, who had recently been admitted to our cottage, was very keen on this new pastime and showed great skill and patience. He was to continue with aero-modelling until he was awarded the gold Duke of Edinburgh Award with aero-modelling as his selection in the hobby section of the award. However, that is another story to be told later.

While all this activity was going on Anne played with the younger boys and somewhat naturally started to take an interest in Dinky toy cars rather than her dolls. However, once the planes reached the flying stage she was quite interested and I had to make her a small 'chuck' glider to fly. Anne was getting along quite happily at her nursery school and taking part in all the activities.

The next excitement would be the 5th of November celebrations, which were of some concern to us as it encouraged the boys to become a little subversive, collecting fireworks and trying to 'improve' them. Also, there were the obvious dangers on firework night. However, they behaved themselves very well, partly because they couldn't afford to purchase fireworks, as they were saving their pocket money up for model kits and loose-leaves for their stamp collection albums. The gardeners had built an enormous bonfire and the boys had asked if they could make a guy for the bonfire. They spent the weekend before the 5th November scrounging old clothes and newspapers to stuff the guy and after a lot of argument decided he was the deputy chief officer! Bonfire night went off without any hitches or accidents. Fireworks were supplied and let off by some local charitable organisation, such as the Round Table. It was a cold but dry evening for the children to enjoy the display and the men were kept busy making sure the children kept at a safe distance.

Back in our winter routine, the model planes were coming along nicely and I expected the boys would complete them during the Christmas holidays. I threw out the thought that it would be nice to enter the annual hobbies inter-cottage competition at Easter. I suggested that they could show off their model aeroplanes and stamp collections and Joan offered to help them practise some cake making. Anne and the younger boys agreed to paint some pictures for the exhibition and soon it was not a question of whether they should enter the competition, but they were talking of winning it! They were a very competitive bunch of youngsters.

Chapter 7

Christmas 1959 and the New Year

The Christmas season for us began with Anne's nativity play at the nursery school. Anne played the part of the Angel Gabriel, and it all went off very well and she appeared to enjoy herself. She enjoyed having the sole attention of her mum and dad. At times, she would get confused about her new life and it showed how important it was to have as much stability for her as we could manage. Chris used to go home most weekends and when we were planning for Anne to go and stay with her grandmother for a few days, she suddenly said, "Of course, this isn't my real home because Grandma's is my real home." She was confused with Chris going away to his real home at weekends and she herself was going to her grandmother's for a few days. I think she thought home was where one went for a few days to stay with relations. It was a bit of a shock to hear she didn't feel it was home where we all lived!

This was our first Christmas working with children in Barnardo's and it was to prove to be the first of many memorable ones, all of which were quite hard work but most rewarding. For children in care it was a difficult time, especially for children not able to visit their own family over the holiday period. For some it was full of unhappy memories. A good deal of sensitivity was required when dealing with some situations. At the same time, they were all children and Christmas with its many activities was an exciting time for them.

The schools broke up a few days before Christmas and the boys now began to take an interest in the kitchen. They took up an invitation to stir the Christmas pudding and have a wish. There was general anticipation towards their forthcoming presents. We suggested that they wrote a letter to Father Christmas with a list, but we had to emphasise that he might not have what they wanted. In fact in those days we had to depend on 'Gifts in Kind' for their presents and not all of these were new. However, the staff in the cottages generously would make up the shortfall. Some of the children had parents and relations who sent them gifts, which were sometimes quite expensive, so we had to discreetly balance things up for the less fortunate. Quite a few of the boys hopefully asked for a model plane kit, thinking that they knew who Father Christmas was going to be.

Christmas Day went off very well and, most important, the 'family' appeared to be well satisfied with their presents. The boys spent the day eating, playing with their presents and watching television, while the staff spent the time cooking, washing-up and dozing in between television programmes.

As the New Year approached, the boys were kept occupied with their presents, either playing with them or building their kits. Plastic model kits of aeroplanes, ships and model railway items were very popular at this time. Then we had a heavy snowfall overnight and the village greens were crowded with children playing in the snow. The boys made a full-size snowman and an enormous snowball, which they proudly displayed outside the front of the cottage. The Christmas holidays soon sped by with model making and a lot of talk about how they could win the hobbies competition at Easter. The model aeroplane makers began to get a little impatient with having to wait for suitable weather for test flying their models.

It was soon time for the children to return to school. We had two new boys who had joined our group during the holidays, as we had two vacancies when Tony and Peter left. One was Charlie who transferred from another cottage to us to be with boys of his own age, and Tom who had a very bad history of continually running away from his previous placements. Fred, now the oldest boy in the cottage, took a more responsible role and was heard to tell Charlie that this was a tidy cottage when Charlie threw a bit of waste paper on the floor. When Tom was 'returned' to the cottage by his social worker for the second time after absconding, Fred told him that he was lucky to be in this cottage. He added that if he went on running away he would end up locked up in an approved school and would have to wear big heavy boots all the time! I am sorry to say that Tom did not take Fred's advice and continued to abscond. Tom was eventually moved to a more secure establishment.

The badminton class continued to expand and was soon full with eight boys and eight girls taking part. The boys all agreed that it was better than PE classes! I now had a problem. Boys from some of the other cottages wanted me to show them how they could make model planes, but I could see it would not be wise for me to interfere with the regime of other cottages. It was a puzzle that I eventually solved by going to see the chief officer. I told him of my dilemma and I asked him how he would feel if I organised a model making class. The house-parents in charge of each cottage would decide which boys came to the class. The chief officer agreed with my suggestion and we worked out a plan. I would take a class once a week for two hours during the winter months in the Wendy hut, where the Brownies had their meetings.

The boys who attended the class proved to be a most happy group who were thrilled to have the opportunity to do something that was quite different. I was allowed the money to purchase two model aeroplane kits and the balsa glue. I had to supply wooden boards to work on, knives to cut the wood and pins and other miscellaneous items. I informed the cottages with older boys who might be interested and I got quite a lot of support from the staff. I thought the only way round would be to let three boys share in the construction of each plane. One boy would make the fuselage, one the wings and the third would be responsible for the tail plane. They duly completed the aeroplanes, which did actually fly, but it was a bit complicated entering them in the inter-cottage hobbies competition! Unfortunately, I did not know at the time that I would not be available the next winter to carry on the class. I don't think there was anyone to take it over. However, I had the satisfaction of knowing that I had introduced the boys to the hobby and it was up to them to carry on by themselves if they so wished.

Life was getting extremely busy but our assistant Joan was getting increasingly competent at handling the older boys and we were able to take our day off each week, and more importantly have time with Anne. Then one day the telephone went and I was informed that the chief officer wanted to see me that morning in his office. I had no idea what to expect. When I arrived at his office, the chief officer made some complimentary remarks regarding my work and then asked me to consider applying for a place on the Home Office course in the residential care of children. The course would last a year and I could start the course in the coming September. This gave us a lot to think about, but we both felt it would be a necessary step if I were to continue in my present career, and I decided to apply for a place.

The chaplain continued with his activities for the older children and as part of his plans to prepare the boys for entry into the Duke of Edinburgh Award Scheme was planning a camp during the Easter holidays. This scheme had three award standards – bronze, silver and gold. From the various options for the bronze level, James had selected camping and map reading, first aid training and the pursuance of a hobby for the boys to follow. The aim of the Easter camp would be to teach the boys camping skills and map reading. The boys were issued with a list of clothing and personal items they would need for this camp. There was one item of clothing that had us all puzzled. It was an 'anorak'. This was something we had never heard of in those days. However, James explained that an anorak was a Scandinavian garment that was loose fitting, waterproof and very suitable for camping. James said he had a supply of these to lend out to campers. The boys, meanwhile, had to be proficient in first aid and had to do a course with St John's Ambulance Brigade, once a week. This entailed lots of practice in bandaging, and the staff were frequently required to be the casualties. The boys had a lot of amusement in 'tying up' the staff.

One day, when I was visiting the model shop for further supplies, the shopkeeper gave me a model railway set for the boys to play with. I suppose it was old stock. It was an 'OO' gauge model railway set made by Trix, consisting of a locomotive, three trucks and a generator. The generator had to be turned by hand and the quicker one turned, the faster the loco ran. One reversed the train by turning the other way. The generator soon wore out and the shopkeeper told me that I could either use batteries or buy a controller to run off the mains. The latter course seemed the most economical, except having invested in the controller, the shopkeeper told me how we could build a permanent model railway. It would be another hobby for the boys and would involve woodwork, and electrical work – fortunately, with only 12 volts – assembling and painting plastic kits and activities such as making grass by dyeing sawdust green for the fields.

Very soon, some of the boys who were not making aeroplanes were helping to start a more permanent and ambitious model railway. I was learning how to build a model railway as we went along with the help of the model shop staff. As I had to fund all the costs of the railway, I made sure that we built everything from as basic materials as we could in order to keep expenses down. This was a good thing as this meant that there was more work for the boys to do and a greater sense of achievement. Also, it meant that progress was slower and this was important as we were short of space. We worked to a design of a low and a high-level station along the top of a low cupboard. This was later extended to an 'L' shape design in the corner of the room. When a temporary length of track on a long board was added to complete the triangle, the trains would be able to make a continuous non-stop run. This saved a considerable amount of space. Later on, the chief officer was impressed when he saw our model railway and promised to see if we could have a room for it in the laundry, which was situated just to the rear of the cottage. However, this offer had to be withdrawn when he realised that other cottages would expect extra space for their activities and little was available.

Meanwhile, Chris and Fred had joined a local youth club, which they enjoyed, and it was good for them to mix with other young persons. However, it so happened that the fashion for young men at that time was to wear very pointed shoes known as 'winkle pickers'. Our two boys felt rather conspicuous in their Barnardo's shoes and asked if they could possibly have a pair of winkle pickers each. We had to get the agreement of the chief officer for this and I am glad to say it was given, but with the proviso that they only wore them when attending the youth club and not round the village. It was important for the boys' self-esteem to feel they did not stand out as 'Barnardo's children' in such critical company.

It was just before Easter when I was summoned to London to appear before a selection panel for the Home Office course, for which I had applied some time previously. The interview went quite well and I was told that if I was successful I would receive a grant from the Home Office towards my keep and expenses. Barnardo's had already warned me that I would not receive any salary from them while I was on the course, but I would receive free board and lodging in return for my help in the cottage at evenings and weekends. I would of course have to hand over my regular duties to other people. In term time, I would be attending the London North West Polytechnic on a daily basis, but there would be three placements in the holiday periods when I would be required to be residential. I knew it would be difficult to get down to studying again. However, I was looking forward to the course and hoping I would be accepted. I was told I should hear from the panel within two or three weeks.

Chapter 8

Easter 1960

As we came near to the end of the Easter term at school, the weather improved and we were able to get outside and fly the model planes. The boys had varied success flying their planes, but some were damaged in the process. Dennis was particularly upset when he launched his plane for its first flight and it seemed to implode, the fuselage completely collapsing under the stress of the tightly wound elastic which powered the propeller. He was in tears but I told him I would help him to repair it when we returned home and it would soon be as good as new. I pointed out to him that he had not glued the balsa wood joints carefully enough.

These trips to Wanstead flats were often made on a Sunday afternoon when the boys were able to watch other enthusiasts flying their planes, as well as flying their own models. Wanstead flats were about two-and-a-half miles away from Barkingside and with only a small car, and 12 boys to transport, as well as up to three staff and, of course, Anne, it was a somewhat daunting task to get everyone there and back. We solved it by sending off five or six boys who walked in the direction of Wanstead flats and I put their precious models in the boot of the car. I then drove some staff and the younger ones direct to the flats and came back to those who were walking and picked them up. I then repeated the exercise to get them home. Anne had a small white ridge tent, which she readily shared with everyone, and it acted as a kind of headquarters or focal point. We kept spare equipment inside as well as the food for our picnic tea.

Life was beginning to get a bit hectic with the hobbies competition, the cross-country races and the Duke of Edinburgh Award camp, all of which had to be fitted in during the Easter holidays. The boys were not showing as much enthusiasm for practising for the annual cross-country races as usual, but they had more exciting things to think about, which would mean new experiences for them. In spite of the diversions, they managed to keep their end up in the cross-country races. Michael came second in the juniors' race. This was not altogether surprising as he was a natural athlete and his headmaster, an international football referee, said that Michael showed a lot of promise at football and might become a professional one day. However, this was not to be as Michael found other interests in his teens. Fred won the seniors' race with some distance to spare and so kept up the tradition of our cottage winning the senior event.

As the day of the hobbies exhibition got nearer, I could feel the excitement building up in our cottage. The younger children were besieging the kitchen and asking to practise their cake making. I think the thought of tasting the end product had something to do with it. The older boys had stopped flying their model planes in order to repair and refurbish the planes, ready for the exhibition.

At last, the great day had arrived. Getting up, washing and dressing took less time than usual on a Saturday morning, as did the washing-up following breakfast. We then all joined in taking the exhibits across to the hall. There was no doubt the eight model planes that flew were spectacular because of their size. At the back of the display we pinned a white sheet to the wall and attached some ten or 12 paintings, mostly done by the younger boys. One of the pictures had been painted by Anne, and she was very thrilled to see it hanging up among the other pictures. In the foreground there were plastic static model planes and ships as well as a wooden model boat. On a separate table we displayed our culinary efforts, which were a great credit to the younger boys. These consisted of a fruitcake, three assorted sponge cakes, a plate of jam tarts and also a plate of currant buns. As soon as we had arranged our entry, we had to leave the hall so that the chief officer and his wife could do the judging. By now the hall was crammed with the various exhibits and we were a bit anxious about our entry compared to the quality of some of the other entries.

It was a long morning for the boys to contain their excitement until we could go back after dinner to the hall and see how well we had done, as well as to view the other exhibits. At last, it was time to return and much to my amazement and to the boys' confident expectations from the beginning, we found we had come equal first with the cottage next door to ours. This cottage was an all-girls cottage that excelled in dress making and cooking. I don't know what the boys would have done if we had been beaten not only by a girl's cottage but also by the cottage next door! I think it was a very fair result although the boys were convinced we had the better display.

No sooner was the hobbies exhibition over than it was time to get ready for the very first camp, practising for the Duke of Edinburgh Award. James the chaplain had decided to concentrate on map reading as well as camping skills. He invited along to the camp ten boys, including four from our cottage, namely Richard, Henry, Dennis and Fred.

James had decided that the first camp would be situated in the grounds of another Barnardo's home, about six miles away, in Epping Forest. This was a home for severely handicapped children and it had very spacious grounds. It was planned that the boys would cycle over there with the chaplain and I would come over in my car loaded with last-minute items including food. Barnardo's would provide the necessary transport of the tents and our personal kit.

The day before the camp the boys were allocated their cycles and spent the time alternately cleaning and adjusting their cycles and testing them out round the green. Meanwhile Eileen and Joan were trying to catch hold of one of the campers at a time, to get them to pack a kit bag of their clothing for the camp, as well as personal items. Some showed a lot of imagination of what they would need for their first camp and wanted to pack a month's supply of clothing "just in case".

The next morning James set off with the ten boys, most of whom were concerned about where they would sleep if the Barnardo's transport failed to turn up. They were even more concerned that I had their picnic lunch in my car and I might lose my way. They were going to discover that their map reading was not necessarily good enough to find their own dinner! All was well, however, and when I arrived, the van was already there with the equipment, which they were busy unloading under James' direction. Having emptied the van, we broke off for dinner. The afternoon was spent putting up the tents, establishing cooking, toilet and washing facilities and, most important, building a campfire. By teatime, they had a healthy appetite and I showed the boys how to make egg fritters.

Some of the older boys had experienced camping at West Runton summer camp whilst some of the younger boys had never been camping at all. They were quite apprehensive, and made even more concerned when the older boys started bragging and told them fabricated tales of their camping experiences. One of the younger boys came up to me and asked if it was true that earwigs crawled into your ears whilst you were sleeping. I quickly assured him that I had never heard of it happening to anyone. I did notice though, that even the older boys gave their tents a careful inspection, using their torches, before scrambling into their beds.

After washing-up, the boys were told to get their beds ready. This was a more difficult task, as Barnardo's had not seen fit to afford sleeping bags yet for the children taking part in the Duke of Edinburgh Award. I think they were wise to wait and see how things developed before spending too much money. The boys were first shown how to lay a ground sheet on the ground and then a folded blanket on top. This was followed by an inner sheet sleeping bag, covered by as many blankets as were available. I had to do the same, as, unlike James, I did not possess a sleeping bag. We then got the campfire going and with a mug of hot cocoa in our hands discussed the plans for the next day. As it was a cold April evening we were very grateful for the warmth from the fire. We completed the evening with traditional campfire songs. Thanks to a day in the open air, the boys were tired and were soon fast asleep.

Next morning I was very glad to get up and start moving around as it had been a frosty night and my makeshift sleeping arrangements had been quite inadequate. I had spent half the night, it seemed, unable to sleep because of the cold. To my surprise, the boys had slept well and didn't complain much about the temperature! After breakfast, when all the chores had been completed, we took the boys to one of the outbuildings belonging to the home, which we had arranged to use. It was as well that we had some cover as it was a wet morning. How lucky we were to have been able to put up the tents in dry weather. We then spent most of the morning explaining the art of map reading using one inch to the mile Ordinance Survey maps. We went back to the camp and after dinner we explained that the boys would put their morning's work to the test.

The boys were going to work in pairs, and were all given the same map reference, a fact of which they were not informed! They were sent off on foot, in pairs and at intervals, to find the map reference and we would be there to meet them. Meanwhile, I set off in my car to purchase some fresh supplies of bread and milk. As I returned to camp, I noticed a group of youngsters marching together through the forest. It was our campers who had decided to pool their resources and share their brainpower. As it defeated the idea of the exercise, I told them to return to camp, if they could find their way! This was a challenge they readily accepted. It would seem that we would have to start all over again.

Spirits were low as they realised that the map reading was an important section of the Duke of Edinburgh Award. If they couldn't manage the map reading, other boys would get the chance to come camping. They really did not want to miss out on the camps, which they liked very much. I think they found camping was a change of routine and enjoyed the relaxed atmosphere.

After tea, we played some physical games with the boys, including a makeshift game of football, which was always a favourite activity. The evening saw the boys cheer up after the disastrous map reading exercise. Afterwards it was time to prepare our beds and light the campfire as dusk was approaching.

We were very puzzled as to how we could persuade the boys to make the effort to learn map reading, an essential part of the Duke of Edinburgh Award. The next day I decided it was time to be cruel to be kind! We gave the lads another short lesson in map reading and carefully arranged them in pairs so that the five best map readers were with a less able partner. Five map references were given to each pair, not necessarily the same, but at one of the references, we would give them their packed lunch. They were told to make the references in the order given. To make it more interesting they were going to do the exercise on their bicycles. Like all boys of that age, they preferred cycling to walking. The exercise was most successful, four pairs finding their packed lunch on time, but we had to meet up with the fifth pair later on to give them a belated lunch. At least we had four boys capable of elementary map reading. The pairs were able to produce, in most cases, evidence that they had found the required references, showing considerable initiative in some instances. One pair brought back a note signed by the local gravedigger to say they had found the church of the given reference. This was the start of my involvement in the Duke of Edinburgh Award Scheme. I am pleased to say Richard went on to attain the gold award in 1966.

We had another two days of camping, which involved some camp craft and more map reading. Time quickly went by and very soon we were loading our equipment onto the van for the return home. I was glad to have a nice warm bed once again as well as to be with Eileen and Anne. The boys were full of their experiences and felt some one-upmanship over those who had not been camping. I decided to save up for a sleeping bag before my next expedition. This brought us to the end of the very busy Easter holidays and one that the boys enjoyed. We now had to get them ready for school.

Chapter 9

Changing Times

It was a few days after the boys had returned to school that I received a rather official looking envelope. It was from the Home Office informing me that I had been selected for the course starting in September at the North Western Polytechnic, situated in north London. After being congratulated by the chief officer I was told that although I would continue to live in the cottage I would have to gradually give up my duties outside the cottage, such as athletics and my model making and badminton classes. Sadly, I would have to give up my involvement with the Duke of Edinburgh Award, just as I was getting very much involved.

The annual village and inter-homes sports came round and went off smoothly. I felt so much more confident organising it for the second time round. Blue Team managed to win the relay race but our village team did not have a great deal of success. I felt that just as I was getting the hang of it I would be handing over the organising of the sports days to someone else.

Auntie Joan announced that, having completed her initial training with us, she had been offered another position with Barnardo's. We were sorry to see Joan leave us but we were happy for her to be offered a job that she fancied. A delightful young lady was in due course introduced to us as a replacement. Auntie Betty was an immediate success with the boys and she fully involved herself in all our activities.

Eileen and I had some long discussions with Miss Golding regarding future plans for our cottage, prompted by my proposed absence for 12 months on the course. The policy within Barnardo's now was to place children in homes where the sexes were mixed rather than in an all-boys or all-girls' unit, as it had been in the past. The proposal was to admit some younger girls into our cottage when we would have several school leavers at the end of the summer term. The idea being that this was an opportune moment to introduce girls into our cottage and at the same time reduce the number of teenage boys while there would not be a man around all the time. Auntie Betty was very pleased with the idea of having some girls in the cottage while Eileen was happy with the proposal and we also felt it would be company for Anne. Anne thought it a great idea and looked forward to having some younger playmates. As I would be away on the course most of the year Eileen was to have an extra assistant trainee house-mother on the staff. Eileen's teaching skills were much appreciated in the training of new staff.

We felt that we would tell the boys about these changes as soon as possible, rather than they find out about these plans through rumours. In due course, we were given agreement to tell the boys of our plans. Needless to say, they were shocked to think of having girls in their cottage. It had been bad enough having Anne, they said, but not more. Their reaction to myself going on a course was quite practical: "That means you will be moving to another home when you finish," they insisted. Some of the boys wanted to know if they could come with us. We said it would not only be our decision, but involved a discussion with Miss Golding and the social workers and their families.

We had a week's break staying with my parents at Colchester. It was during this week that Anne went down with mumps, fortunately not too seriously. However, she was convinced that she had caught it from Grandmother's pillow! It seemed logic to her that the pillow was the source of infection as she had been quite healthy when she went to bed. However, I was to be less fortunate and when I woke up in the morning a few days later I could feel a lump in my neck and I knew I had not caught it from my pillow! I had quite a high temperature and each morning Eileen would take my temperature and give me an edited version of what it was, so as not to alarm me. Then she would go into breakfast and the boys would want to know what my temperature was reading. They would then say, "And what does Uncle think it is?" They obviously felt good knowing something I did not know and a touch of sympathy I would hope! As my temperature failed to go down, I was taken into the village hospital. I had one unofficial visitor after I had been there a few days. Dennis crawled underneath and around the hospital until he could find the room I was in and tapped on the window when he found the right room. I was not feeling well enough to appreciate his visit. I soon recovered after my treatment in hospital but it took a long time to recover my strength and energy.

Meanwhile our activities were mainly a repeat of the previous years. I had managed to get Arthur a small plot of ground to have as a garden and he obviously derived tremendous pleasure from it. I think he found it nice to have his own space. I wish I had thought of encouraging more of the boys to have a garden. I had a cine-camera, which I used mainly for taking pictures on our holidays and of Anne's activities. I had been taking pictures of her at nursery school and their end of term's frolics. She would be going to an infants' school next term. I suddenly thought I must make some films of the village homes before I had to move on. The boys used to love watching my holiday films that I had previously made. They never appeared to tire of seeing the same films and especially enjoyed announcing what was going to happen next!

Summer holidays were with us again, but it was not causing so much concern this time as we were more in control of the situation and the boys were more settled. This year we were going to the West Runton camp for the second fortnight and the deputy would be in charge. Auntie Janet had now joined our cottage and would be coming to the summer camp with the rest of us. The camp followed the well established routine of previous years, but I found playing games with the boys was really hard work, as I hadn't fully regained my strength after having had mumps.

The previous year I had taken an ordinary hurricane lamp to light up our tent, but we found the light rather dim. This year I took a Tilley lamp that worked on paraffin oil under pressure and had to be started using methylated spirits. It gave out a much better light in our tent and also was an asset in the evening when the staff gathered in the kitchen tent for a hot drink and a little relaxation before turning in for the night. It transpired that the deputy had brought his own Tilley lamp and gave me the job of refuelling it each day. When he saw I also had one, he said, "I hope you are not using my fuel to fill your lamp." I took it as a joke but I was not so sure that it was intended as one.

Next door to our camp each year was a camp for disadvantaged children, run by some association of the public schools. One of the highlights of the week was to play a 'wide game', which involved the staff returning to the camp during the day without being recognised by the children in the camp. All sorts of disguises were used and, of course, the staff had to do something different each year. I was approached by Fred, one of the staff, asking me to help him out. The plan was that he had borrowed the costume of a cartoon figure called 'Flook' that appeared in one of our daily newspapers. The costume included a head-piece, which completely enclosed his head, and so was an excellent disguise. Fred wanted my assistance to make it look more authentic. I was to accompany him posing as a reporter advertising the newspaper and giving away free copies. Fred then wanted me to round up some of the children in our camp who would follow behind enjoying the spectacle. I had very little difficulty in getting volunteers, especially when they found that they were part of the secret.

I arranged to meet Fred with my troupe of children in the car park in the village where he would change into his costume. We would proceed to the campsite via an indirect and not too obvious route. I was wearing a raincoat and hat and tried to look like a newspaper reporter. Fred presented me with a newspaper satchel containing a number of copies of the newspaper. As we went on our way, we encountered several 'suspect' figures that I guessed were on a similar task as ourselves. These characters included three Roman Catholic Fathers, two telephone engineers complete with a ladder and a young lady with a shopping basket, who looked a bit suspect. Most original of all was a toilet tent that, when no one was looking, moved slowly away from a nearby caravan and in the direction of the camp. I suppose the occupant intended to make a sudden dash for the camp when he got near enough to see the boys who were defending had their attention distracted.

As we walked along the road from the village, several cars stopped and asked what was going on. I told them it was Flook and they could read all about it in the paper that I was giving to them. Other cars saw me giving away free newspapers, stopped their cars and held their hands out for one. It was only afterwards that I realised I had been giving away yesterday's papers! Obviously, Fred had a sense of economy. Meanwhile, the boys who were playing the role of camp followers were thoroughly enjoying themselves as part of the act. As we made a casual approach to the camp we were challenged, but the boys guessed the wrong identification, which was hardly surprising, as they could not see inside the rather grotesque costume, which completely enclosed Fred. A few more yards and Fred had achieved the object of entering the camp unchallenged in his rightful name. After many thanks from Fred for all our help, we went back to our camp where we related our various experiences. I was pleased we had been asked to participate and it was a good experience for our boys.

And so what was to be my last camp at West Runton came to an end. As we were the second camp this year, we had to take down the tents and help load them on the lorry. Meanwhile, we had loaded our car to the roof and beyond – we now had a roof rack – so it was now a question of watching the springs! The bus arrived to take the children back to the village and we set off in our car, which did not let us down and we arrived safely back at Woodside. Anne was pleased to be home once more.

It was soon time to get the boys back to school and much to their amusement Uncle Butler would soon be going to 'school' as well.

Our cottage and car

Daily tent inspection at West Runton camp

West Runton camp dining marquee with Eileen serving

Tea on the green outside our cottage

Start of the model railway

Challenge Club - camp fire

Two aunties having a trip along the coast

Chapter 10

Back to School

At eight o'clock on a Monday morning towards the end of September, a rather apprehensive figure was waiting at the local underground station. I was clutching my new leather briefcase, complete with sandwiches, and trying to look at ease amongst all the other commuters. I was wondering what I had let myself in for, as I knew it would be hard to return to college and study after such a long time. When I had found my way to the college and had been directed to the room I was to attend, I found myself in a large lecture hall where there were already some 20 people chatting in small groups. I soon discovered that we were all equally apprehensive!

Shortly after my arrival, a lady with grey hair and a German accent came into the room. She announced that her name was Miss Becker and that she would be our course tutor. I found that I was the only student from Barnardo's although there were quite a few from other voluntary homes. The remainder of my fellow students were from local authority run homes, chiefly London County Council homes. The day seemed to flash by and in no time at all I was standing on the platform waiting to start my homeward journey. Eileen, and not least the boys, wanted to hear about my day. Anne could not really understand why her daddy had to go to school but was pleased to see that I had come back home. Eileen and I wanted to compare our first day of our new routine that would last for a year. I was very concerned about the extra load I was placing on Eileen, leaving her suddenly with a lot of responsibility and having very little chance to discuss any problem situations together, as we had been able to do in the past. It was a good job that I had not been set any homework to do on that first evening as it would have been hard to find the time to complete it. When I had managed to eat my tea and answer all the questions, it was nearly time for bed.

I was quite glad when Friday evening came and I had two days break. It could not be described as a rest with eight boys wanting some attention. Back at college, I was beginning to get more homework but sometimes I found I could share it with the boys, thus killing two birds with one stone. We were all expected to complete a study of some aspect of the course during the year and I chose child art. We were getting lectures in child art and child drama and so I soon encouraged the boys to paint some pictures for me to use on the course. I also bought a Leroy Anderson record of music that the child art lecturer had recommended and soon had the boys acting out their feelings to music. They entered these strange activities with some enthusiasm. I think they were glad to receive some of my attention at weekends.

One day we were taken on a trip to the other side of London to a school of puppetry where we were introduced to the world of puppets. We were shown how to make glove puppets using papier-mâché for the heads. Back at college, we practised making puppets and were told how to make a puppet theatre. Meanwhile Miss Becker surprised us by saying that it was an expectation of the course that we would give a Christmas party to all the lecturers who were involved on our course. The party would be on the last day of the Christmas term. The idea behind this was to give us practice at organising similar events for children. We decided to give a puppet show at the party as part of the entertainment, and I volunteered to organise this part of the activities.

I designed a folding puppet theatre that would fit into my car and I was able to make this at weekends with some help from the boys. What to do with our puppets became the next question as we didn't seem to have any budding playwrights volunteering. Then someone had a brilliant idea – we would do a show featuring the members of staff and perhaps get our own back for having to give this party. It was dangerous territory. It was to be hoped that they had a sense of humour!

When I got home that night I told the boys about our decision to do the puppet show about the staff and that I was making a lot of the puppets. They were tickled pink about the whole idea of making puppets of the staff and readily offered to help. Firstly, I made a puppet of the child drama lecturer – he had a large red beard. The puppets had to be easily identifiable and in some ways were more of a caricature than a true likeness. Next, we 'made' the art lecturer. He was a chain smoker and so we gave him a 'built in' wooden cigarette fixed to his left hand. Hair for their heads was always a bit of a problem, but when I came to model our tutor, Miss Becker, Dennis had a brilliant idea; he suggested steel wool for her hair. They all enjoyed the idea of our teacher having what was basically kitchen utensil cleaning material for her hair. Actually, I thought it most effective and quite realistic. For the other puppets, we used strands of wool. We had some offers of help with the clothing from the lady members of the staff in the cottage, which was gladly accepted by the boys and myself.

Christmas was soon on the horizon and so was the end of term party for the staff at college. Hurried rehearsals at our lunch break had to suffice for our puppet show while some of our colleagues set to work to plan some suitable party games and competitions and others sorted out the catering arrangements.

The last day of term finally arrived. We had all day to prepare for the event, which was scheduled to commence at five o'clock when the staff who had been invited would have finished work for the day. I think the highlight of the evening was the puppet show although we had much apprehension regarding how the show would appeal to the staff, especially the tutors whom we had tried to portray. When those of us, the puppeteers, entered the back of the little theatre we found that someone had encouragingly chalked 'Abandon hope all who enter here!' on the back of the stage. Once we had started, I noticed that the lecturers whom we were portraying were watching their counterparts intently. I noticed that Miss Becker appeared quite fascinated with her character and had a smile on her face. What a relief! I think it was a new experience to find 'themselves' on the stage. We were then congratulated for the party and I think we could be assured that we had all gained some good marks for our efforts.

We now had a week's holiday over the Christmas period before we spent the rest of the Christmas vacation in a residential placement. I was pleased to get back to Woodside where the staff, and to a lesser extent the boys, were busily preparing for Christmas. Everyone was pleased that the puppets had been successful and wondered what my next escapade would be. Christmas Day was a very similar event to our first one, but I think we had improved a little in our organisation and the party later in the day was a great success and was enjoyed by all. Eileen's cousin Richard, a 19-year-old, came to stay with us over the holiday and was an instant hit with the older boys. Because of the relatively small age gap, they related very well with him and he joined enthusiastically in with the activities.

Chapter 11

Staying the Course

Once Christmas was over it was not long before I was packing my bags for my three weeks' placement in a reception and assessment centre situated in the East End of London. As I already worked in a voluntary organisation, all my placements were to be in local authority run units. Once again, I was apprehensive about leaving Eileen on her own to run the cottage, especially keeping the boys occupied during the school holidays. It was different during the previous term time when I was there to support her in the evenings and weekends. Eileen told me later that it was at this time that she felt the weight of responsibility most heavily. She felt very alone as she closed the door after seeing me off and wondered how the boys would react now they knew that I would not be around. For my part, I did not fancy being parted for even three weeks from Eileen and Anne. I felt more like a visitor in the cottage and things were happening over which I no longer had any chance to have my say. This was a difficult time for both of us.

The assessment centre had three self-contained groups of children, boys up to 11 years of age, boys of 12 years old and upwards and a girls' group. This establishment only catered for children who were admitted for assessment. This meant that they would be there for a few months, during which time they would be carefully observed by the staff and seen by the educational psychologist. This would be followed by a case conference held to decide the best possible placement for the child. The meeting would be attended by the social worker who was involved with the family, the psychologist and members of staff from the centre. I was allocated to the older boys' group, as the house-mother for that group was taking the place of the cook, who was on holiday. The deputy superintendent was in charge of this group. It was hard work to keep the boys occupied as it was the time of the Christmas holidays and the weather was atrocious, giving little opportunity to take the boys out.

Eventually, it was time to return home for a long weekend before returning to college and once more settling into our term time routine. Eileen and I shared our experiences of the last few weeks and I was glad to hear that all had gone well at Woodside. The boys had gone back to school for the spring term and were getting over the shock of a lovely little family of four young girls coming to our cottage. The oldest was nine years old and mothered her three younger sisters. I could see that they quite stole the hearts of the young staff. We made sure Anne did not feel too put out because the girls were bound to get a lot of attention as the staff tried to settle them in. In the long term, I was sure that Anne would enjoy some playmates.

On return to the college we all swapped tales of our placements; some slightly exaggerated, I felt. It was good to be back. I was getting very interested in my project of child art and enjoyed exploring all the different avenues involved. I learnt that it was necessary to judge child art on its own terms.

Back at Barkingside James had decided to call the Duke of Edinburgh Award group 'The Challenge Club' and it was open to all boys and girls aged 13 years and upwards. Considerable progress had been made including a supply of sleeping bags for the coming Easter and summer camps! The first boys had completed their bronze awards by early spring and in the beginning of March they received their awards. Out of the seven boys who won their awards, I was pleased to know that two of our boys, Henry and Richard, had achieved their award. A member of Barnardo's council came down to present the awards, which were the first gained by the Challenge Club. Much to my regret, I was unable to be present owing to my college commitments. At the college, we were all wondering where we would be going for our Easter placements. I was quite pleased to find that I had been placed in a long-stay home for 30 children in the Lincolnshire countryside. It would be a very different experience to my previous one.

As soon as the college broke up for Easter, and before my placement in Lincolnshire, Eileen and I were invited to Barnardo's headquarters at Stepney Causeway in London for an interview with two of Barnardo's senior staff. Finding that we had made good time in our trusty little car, I decided, very foolishly as it turned out, to drive past the assessment centre to show Eileen where I had recently been working. This centre was only about half a mile off my route but unfortunately, as I turned back for Stepney Causeway, I managed to get on the road for the Blackwall Tunnel and there was no escape! I told Eileen not to worry, we would just have to drive through the tunnel and come back again in ten minutes. Little did I know that there had been an accident in the northbound tunnel and when we emerged there was an endless stationary queue for that tunnel. I tried not to sound too worried as I explained plan B to Eileen. I said we would go along the river towards the centre of London and cross the Thames using the Rotherhythe Tunnel. I kept my fingers crossed that this tunnel was functioning normally and the traffic was flowing. It would be too late to use plan C, if one existed, in the face of further hold-ups. Much to my relief traffic appeared to be flowing normally when we got to the tunnel. We were lucky and arrived at Stepney Causeway dead on time but without any time to brush ourselves down and take a deep breath. I was not very popular with Eileen but at least we did not keep anyone waiting.

At the interview, we were told that the purpose of the meeting was to plan for our future when I had completed my present course. It was suggested that a home for 32 children near Canterbury in Kent had a vacancy for a superintendent and matron. The home had run as a nursery for several years with a matron in charge but was now to cater for children of all ages. We said we were very interested but would like to see the home first of all, before we accepted the appointment. We said we wanted to see the layout of the place and the possibilities it held and to be sure we felt it was the right place for us. Although there was a sense of surprise that we didn't jump to accept the promotion, it was agreed that they would arrange a visit before I went off on my Easter placement.

We went back home very excited and wanted so much for this home near to Canterbury to be the right place for us. It sounded just right but we needed to make sure. Miss Golding and the chief officer congratulated us on our promotion, subject of course to our visit and acceptance. Miss Golding said it was time to tell the staff and children. The reaction of most of the boys was that they had seen it all before. Our predecessors had been promoted to go in charge of a Barnardo's home in the south of England. There were three boys who said they wanted to come with us, who did not have any local 'roots'. It was arranged that on Monday of the next week, before I went to my practical placement in Lincolnshire, Eileen, Anne and I and the three boys would visit the Canterbury home. The boys were Dennis and Charlie, both 14 years old, and Jimmy, who had been more recently admitted to our cottage.

Straight after breakfast on that Monday morning three excited boys squeezed into the back seat of our car. Both Eileen, with Anne on her lap, and I also felt the sense of adventure. I was not going to risk getting held up in tunnels and so we drove via the Woolwich free ferry, which we negotiated safely. We were expected to arrive in time for lunch but first of all traffic delayed us and then we had to find the home, which was called Chilton Park.

Chilton Park was a listed building, standing in its own grounds and approached by a long drive through parkland, where cows and sheep grazed. It was in a truly lovely rural setting, and we drove up the drive to this country mansion. The boys were clearly impressed, as they put on their best behaviour. We apologised for our late arrival and were told that the children had already started having their dinner. We were asked if we would like to join them in the dining room, and we readily agreed. Much to my surprise when we entered the dining room, all the children politely stood up. I felt quite embarrassed, not being used to such formality, whilst the boys could hardly keep straight faces. I gave them a glare, which I hoped would help to stifle their oncoming laughter and perhaps remind them that I might encourage such politeness if I came here! We had been offered the post of superintendent and matron and intended to accept the offer, all being well, once we had made our visit. The boys knew this was the situation and they only had to make their own decision as to whether they wished to come with us if we accepted the posts.

Time was too short to take in everything in such a quick visit. Our main objectives were to see what the possibilities for childcare were, and especially for working with older children and what accommodation was available for children and staff. Our own accommodation was somewhat limited, having a sitting room on the ground floor and two bedrooms and a bathroom on the first floor, which were not self-contained. Anne was pleased to find that her bedroom would be a little larger than her previous one. We were not disappointed to find both our bedroom and sitting room would be a little larger. After being shown round the main house and the grounds, we were offered a welcome cup of tea. Chilton Park had been a home for younger children and because of a change of policy, it had been run more recently as an all-age unit. Some of the young children had been allowed to remain as they grew up rather than being transferred to a home for older children. Of some concern to us was that the home had been given two ponies and a trap, and neither Eileen nor I knew anything about caring for these animals.

The journey going home seemed to be over very quickly as we all had so much to think about. All three boys were soon discussing what they had seen and readily hoped that they would be coming, and looked forward to living in the country. Anne was tired after a long day and slept most of the journey. We would have to wait until the next day to hear her verdict. To our relief, Anne decided that she would like to go to Canterbury, but I felt her choice was coloured by the thought of the ponies. We told her that we could not manage the ponies unless there was a member of staff and some of the older children who knew how to care for them. Eileen and I knew that we had a lot to think about but felt it was the right move for us, although clearly it would be a great challenge for us both. We did not have much time to make a decision, as I was due shortly to go off to Lincolnshire for my practical placement, but we decided to go ahead and accept the appointment that we had been offered, and would take up the positions when I finished my course. If any of the three boys definitely decided that they wanted to come with us they would have to await a meeting with Miss Golding, their social worker, and any concerned member of their family, before a final decision could be made.

I was very concerned that I was leaving Eileen with most of the planning and arrangements to make as well as the cottage to run without my support. However, I knew she had gained confidence from coping during my last placement and that she was a capable organiser. In fact, most important of all, we felt we must ensure that the children did not feel insecure with all the changes in the cottage. The change of home would affect Anne, of course, who was about to 'lose' her daddy again at the mysterious school he kept attending.

I decided to take my car with me to Lincolnshire and this would give me a chance to explore the countryside on my day off, assuming that I would get one or two during my four-week placement. Just before dark, after a long drive, I arrived at the home set in a very rural part of Lincolnshire. The instructions given to me were very good and I found it without too much trouble. I arrived at a lovely country house, set in its own grounds, where I was greeted by the superintendent and his wife. The children's home was a long-stay establishment run by the local authority for boys and girls.

It transpired that the full-time gardener had to have an operation at the local hospital, and as I had previously trained in horticulture, they wanted me to replace the gardener as much as possible, as well as working with children. I could see I was going to be busy! The children were of mixed age range, predominately at the older end of the scale, and were quite friendly and were obviously used to students doing their placements there. A favourite pastime of the children was croquet, which was played on a fairly large stretch of lawn, but because of its shape, the hoops were laid out in a rather unorthodox pattern. Each time the lawn was mown, now one of my jobs, the hoops were laid differently, which made the games more interesting for the children. It was very popular and the children obviously got a lot of pleasure from it. It would, I thought, be a suitable game to have at Chilton Park.

When the children's officer visited the home, I think she must have been impressed with my gardening. She suggested that I might like to apply for the post of superintendent of a similar children's establishment, also set in the country, when I completed my course in five months' time. It had a reputation for its colourful and well-kept grounds. Did she think she could save money by having a combined post of superintendent/gardener, I wonder? Of course, I told her that I already had a job promised by Barnardo's when the course was finished. Four weeks soon sped by and it was time to return home and back to the final term of the course. It had been a very interesting experience, especially as it was a very similar establishment to Chilton Park and the couple in charge had a lot of experience.

It was great to be back with my family and we had so much to plan and think about. Eileen had been great, keeping the cottage running smoothly and making decisions for both of us regarding our move to Canterbury. As the present superintendent of Chilton Park would be leaving during August and I would not complete my course until October, it had been decided that Eileen would have to go ahead and take charge of Chilton Park in August. This would enable the children to start the autumn school term on time. I would follow in October. In preparation, Eileen would go down to the home in June for two weeks in order to 'learn the ropes'. Apart from ensuring the smooth running of the establishment there was a lot of bookkeeping and paperwork involved.

Before we left Barkingside for good, I would have my summer leave from my course and we decided that we would take the eight boys, four young girls and all the staff to the seaside for a week, with Barnardo's approval. We could not all go to the West Runton camp because it was for older children only. We booked a church hall in Eastbourne for a week and as it was our last time together for many of us, it seemed a fitting way of saying goodbye.

A big Barnardo's van took all of our luggage and an old mattress for each of us, as well as games and cooking utensils etc. The children and the staff went by train and Eileen, Anne and I drove down in our car. The mattresses would be placed directly on the floor of the church hall and covered with blankets and sheets. The ladies and girls slept on the stage, whilst I slept with the boys on the floor of the main hall. With the stage curtains drawn, we had the advantage of two separate rooms. Toilets were a bit limited as were washing facilities. Kitchen facilities were equally limited. We took sandwiches for our lunches and one day bought fish and chips for our high tea, which was a treat for everyone, particularly the cooks!

The weather stayed fine and we all had a very happy, memorable holiday. The girls loved the sandy beaches and a visit to a miniature village, whilst the boys enjoyed football on the beach and slot machines on the pier. One day Eileen, Anne and I were enjoying our lunch together on the beach with the eight boys when an elderly lady sitting nearby, who had been watching us with some fascination, said to Eileen, "Oh, my dear – are they all yours?" Eileen gave a very definite negative answer. I think the lady must have had a vivid imagination as one boy was of African origin and another was of Chinese origin and one boy had very brilliant ginger hair, and none of the boys looked like brothers!!

All too soon, it was time for us to return to Barkingside and start packing for our move to Chilton Park. There was a great sense of excitement, tinged with sadness, as we started saying farewell to some of the 'Woodside' children and to staff and friends in the village.

Once again, I had to leave Eileen to organise things on her own, as I had to start my final placement with Kent County Council. I was to be placed in two of their homes in East Kent, not far from Chilton Park. Miss Becker thought that this would be a useful placement, as in the future I would be working closely with that authority, as they had placed children at Chilton Park.

Part Two:

Chilton Park

Chapter 12

New Beginnings

As I was starting my final six weeks' placement in Kent, Eileen was finishing working in the village. Having seen the furniture van off to Chilton Park with all our worldly goods, Eileen and Anne accompanied by three excited boys took the underground train to Victoria station and the train to Canterbury. Dennis, Charlie and Jimmy had all been allowed to come with us to Canterbury and I think they felt they were 'one up' on 'Uncle' by going to Chilton Park ahead of me.

I spent the first three weeks of my practical placement in a home for 20 long-stay children on the North Kent coast. For the remaining three weeks, I worked in a home that consisted of eight separate units for long-stay children. Each unit had a capacity for ten or 12 boys and girls. I was asked to work in any unit that was short-handed and in one case, I had to take the place of a cleaner who was on sick leave. I also worked with the relief house-mother, who took over the running of a unit while the house-parents had a day off.

While I was working in this establishment, I was able to live at Chilton Park as Eileen was now in residence and I could drive to work daily. It was nice to be able to give her some support and spend time with Anne. We were now very excited with our new jobs and were longing to get going together when I finished my course. Chilton Park had been closed for the summer holidays. The very young children had been moved to more suitable permanent placements. The older children had been sent to other homes "for a holiday" during this period and returned to Chilton Park in time to start school at the beginning of the autumn term.

On arriving at Chilton Park, the immediate problem for Eileen was the two ponies. There were not any of the staff left who were interested or had the expertise to look after the ponies, and finding herself already short of staff, Eileen had to give her priority to looking after the children. Barnardo's arranged for the ponies to go to another home where they would be well looked after.

The main problem at Chilton Park was going to be the shortage of staff. The deputy and his wife had moved to Barkingside to take over our cottage in the village. Some of the other staff preferred to work with younger children and had already transferred to another home. I was not due to finish my course until October. Furthermore, I had persuaded two of my fellow students, Bill and Mary, to apply to Barnardo's for the posts of deputy and house-mother respectively at Chilton Park. We all got along well together and had similar ideas and so I was extremely happy to have them 'on board'. This meant that we were temporarily three senior staff short until the middle of October. Miss Roots, our new boss, was tickled pink at the idea of sending off one of their staff for training and getting three trained staff back.

On completion of our practical placements, we all had to return to college at the end of September for our final three weeks. I was able to travel up to London by train each day and I was so happy not to have any more time spent away from home. We were all excited about starting new jobs and talking about our experiences in our placements. Bill and Mary wanted to know all about Chilton Park and catch up with the latest news. Most importantly, we had all passed the course except for two ladies who had dropped out soon after Christmas. Bill had hurt his back climbing out of the swimming pool on the last day of his placement and was in a lot of pain. Bill would join us in a few days and Mary had arranged to have a week's break before coming down to Canterbury.

On the last day of the course, I made an early start and took my car up to London, so as to bring back all my college work. We had all agreed to have a meal out in a London restaurant on that last evening and it was already ten o'clock on a very windy night when I set off for Canterbury, a tired but happy man. Fortunately, I was not too merry, because student allowances did not encourage too much spending on alcohol! I was just about able to keep my eyes open as I drove up the half-mile drive at Chilton Park, at about 1am, when to my horror I saw an enormous tree lying across the drive completely blocking my way. Nothing could be done about this until morning so I had to leave my car, clamber over the tree and walk up the rest of the drive. I knew what my first job would be in the morning! No, I did not have to clear the drive. I did not have a chain saw, but I knew a man who would have one. I contacted the farmer who kept his cattle in the park. He was most helpful and soon had the obstruction removed.

After a few days of sorting out some problems, which required our immediate attention, Eileen and I decided to have a walk all round the house and grounds to note in detail exactly what facilities were available. We had to consider any changes we would like to make to meet the needs of older children, now the home was no longer to serve as a nursery. Our priority was to see how we could make three rooms suitable as self-contained group rooms as 'home' for about 12 children in each, and provide a staff room and an office

As soon as the children were safely transported to school, we began our tour, starting off at the front door, which opened into a large oak-panelled hall. To the right was a door to a room currently used as a playroom. This room was about the right size for one of the groups. It was a bright room, having plenty of windows. Just past this playroom was a room used as a dining room for all the children and staff who were on duty. This room was very large and as we looked at it we thought it could easily be sectioned off to make a more homely group room, and also provide a smaller room behind which could serve as a staff room. The boot room and the toilets were situated behind this area.

Down the corridor to the left was a very pleasant room, at present used as a staff room. We thought this would make an ideal group room and make a home for the third group. We wondered how the staff would like being moved from this lovely room, and knew this could be one of the next problems we had to face. Opposite this room were the laundry room and the kitchen. The laundry room was quite a good size but smaller than the group rooms. This room was used by the seamstress, Miss Ashton, whom Eileen had already discovered ruled both the children and staff. Next to this room was the kitchen. Here stood a large Aga cooker, which provided the sole means of cooking for the household. There were sinks and cupboards all round the walls but in the centre was the largest kitchen table I have ever seen! It was covered in sheets of red Formica and dominated the room. This room was ruled by the cook, Mrs Green, and we were told that children were not allowed in there. We would see! Leading down from the kitchen were stairs to the basement where there were two wine cellars and a large boiler room, which housed two large coke-fired boilers – one for the central heating and the other for the domestic hot water. The tools for the boilers were 6ft long or more and I understood from the gardener, Mr Green, that he looked after the boilers except for a final top-up of fuel before we went to bed, a job Bill and I would share. The coke was delivered once a year when a complete railway truckload was ordered, and delivered by a lorry from Canterbury station. On emerging from the cellars and coming out of the kitchen, we turned right and passed various small rooms, some used for general food storage and some for washing-up and for laundry purposes. The only remaining room on the ground floor was our sitting room, next to the back stairs, which led to the two upper floors.

It was now time for a cup of coffee and a chance to mull over what we had seen before looking at the next floor. Refreshed by the break, we went back along the corridor past the laundry and sewing room to the very impressive main staircase, which was situated opposite the entrance hall. Turning left at the top of the stairs, we encountered the largest room in the house, the ballroom! It was a truly beautiful room with a large curved bay window along one side and a lovely decorated ceiling. It was two storeys high occupying part of the second floor as well. It was divided by wooden partitions into three bedrooms for children. We felt that this was a most unsatisfactory use of the room. There wasn't any feeling of homeliness about it and we felt that we needed to change this. Somehow, we had to find more bedroom accommodation and a lot of thought needed to go into the use we made of this lovely room. The rest of this floor was taken up with one staff bedroom, several bedrooms for four to six children, bathrooms and our accommodation, which consisted of our bedroom, a small one for Anne, and a bathroom. The top floor, which was reached by the back stairs, was used as staff accommodation. The rooms were rather small and had sloping ceilings.

After a short lunch break, we started our tour round the grounds and decided first of all to look at the properties that adjoined the main drive to the house. At the beginning of the drive was the lodge house; at present, it was unoccupied but we noted that it could be used for staff accommodation. Walking back along the half-mile long drive, we had parkland on both sides as well as a small cricket ground used by a local club. Just after passing the cricket ground, a path on the left side led a cottage where Mr and Mrs Green, lived. A short distance further on was the dower house, originally built for the widow of the owner of the property to enable the heir to take over the main house. This building was now being used for staff accommodation. Continuing onwards for another 200-300yds, the main drive swept to the right in front of the main entrance to the house. At this point, the drive narrowed and we continued up the drive past the house where we came to a building almost hidden by the trees. To our amazement, it turned out to be a squash court that was in excellent condition and complete with good electric lighting. This was obviously going to be a very useful resource but at present it was filled with discarded furniture and two table tennis tables, both in need of repair. Just past the squash court were the original stables, now used as garages for staff cars and the Barnardo's 12-seat minibus.

We walked behind the outbuildings at the back of the house where there was a walled kitchen garden. It appeared that the gardener held the only key and the gate was always kept locked. Very convenient for the gardener, but not for me! Another area as yet not seen for our concern. A small wood was situated at the back of this garden, which led down to a disused railway line. We continued round to the farther side of the house and entered a wood of about three acres, in which the children were free to roam. We had been told that tree climbing was forbidden as one of the older girls had fallen from a tree and broken both of her wrists. We did not feel that this was the right decision and would consider allowing the children to climb the trees. We felt that there was more chance of an accident through them climbing the trees surreptitiously than if it was allowed, and it was good for the children to get their excitement in a 'legal' manner. As we came out of the wood, we were surprised to find a hard tennis court in good condition and surrounded by wire netting. This was indeed a useful resource for the older children. We now found ourselves back on the wide drive in front of the house. The drive was surrounded by neatly cut grass and one or two flowerbeds, and in a fenced-off area there was a large but shallow paddling pool.

We went back into the house for the inevitable cup of tea. We had so much to think about and to discuss with Bill and Mary as soon as they arrived, as well as with the other staff, but now it was time to concentrate our thoughts and energy towards the children who would shortly be returning from school.

Chapter 13

So Much to Do

We soon found ourselves busy collecting gifts of fruit and vegetables in the minibus from the Harvest Festival services held in the local churches. We were very grateful for these gifts, which supplemented the produce that Mr Green grew in the garden as we were a big 'family' of 32 children and 11 resident staff. When possible, both Eileen and I would go together not only to help carry the produce back to the minibus, but it was an opportunity to introduce ourselves. It seemed the local people had got used to a matron being in charge in recent times and assumed that Eileen was in charge. Well, I don't think they had the slightest idea that I existed! This caused some rather amusing incidents during our first year at Chilton Park.

Bill arrived later in October, closely followed by Mary, and just as we were thinking we were sufficiently well staffed to get on with the changes we had in mind, we found that we were without a cook. At this time it was not surprising that one or two of the children were enuretic. On this particular morning, the soiled bed linen was placed in one of the scullery sinks that was used for washing-up and not in the bowl that was provided. There was not time to remedy matters until after breakfast and so Eileen told the children they would have to wash up in the kitchen. A few minutes later and Mrs Green arrived and quickly came out of the kitchen, running after

Eileen and telling her in no uncertain terms that if the children came into the kitchen, then she would have to go. Eileen replied, "I am sorry Mrs Green but the children will have to come into the kitchen until I have time to see to the washing and disinfect the sink." The cook picked up her coat and bag and stormed out of the kitchen. As people rarely like changes to routine, the inevitable changes that we were making would have a somewhat negative effect on the established staff, both domestic and childcare. It was important that we made the changes seem positive to the children. We did not see Mrs Green again in the kitchen. She said she would only come back if the children were not allowed in the kitchen. It was time for the staff to understand who was in charge, and we were fully supported in this by the senior officers. It was unfortunate that the cook felt she had to go and could not adapt to change. It also meant that Eileen, with some help from the staff, had all the cooking to do.

We had our first staff meeting and discussed the proposed changes to the rooms. As was to be expected, the old staff were less than enthusiastic while the new staff were fully in favour. In the end, it was accepted that dividing the children into three family groups, consisting of ten to 12 children, would give them the security that they needed and at the same time, we could give them more individual attention. We had three large natural families at Chilton Park, it being the policy to use the larger size home to enable the whole family of siblings to grow up together under one roof. It was suggested that in the case of the family of eight, we might keep the group better balanced to divide the family between two groups. The groups would eat their meals in their group rooms and we would endeavour to keep the groups together in the bedrooms as well. We decided not to make any changes until after Christmas.

One morning we had a telephone call from the local Round Table, asking for the matron! They informed us that they would be giving us a firework display as usual. Apparently, they supplied and let off fireworks in the park beside a bonfire that the gardener prepared. It was the established custom for them to bring their wives and children along to enjoy the show and we supplied some sandwiches and hot drinks. I had a word with the gardener, who was most co-operative in spite of his wife having walked out of her job. He said he would contact the farmer's tractor driver and he would collect the big broken branches that fell off the trees in the park and help build up the bonfire. When it was finished, the bonfire looked enormous, some 15ft high, but the children were not so impressed. In fact, every year when they saw the finished bonfire they claimed it was not as big as the previous year. Perhaps it was something to do with growing taller themselves!

Before 5th November arrived, one of the older boys decided that he would celebrate the event on his own by blowing up the kitchen – well, not quite! Tom had been looking rather furtive lately and I put it down to the fact that he quite naturally resented newcomers coming to his home and ordering him about. I had only come back from my course in the last two or three weeks and had very little time to get to relate meaningfully with all the children. Eileen, who was temporarily doing the cooking, saw Tom emerging from the cellar and he mumbled something about helping Uncle. The next day Eileen saw him going down the cellar steps from the kitchen and came to check with me that I knew what he was doing in the cellar. I immediately entered the cellar quietly and I came across Tom, looking rather suspicious. When I asked him what was he doing, he showed me a small brass model of an army field gun on wheels about 6in long. He had filled the barrel with the contents of a firework he had taken apart, and then into the barrel he had rammed a projectile of some sort. He had fitted a fuse to the gunpowder and was just about to light it! I explained to him that at best, the projectile might have come out of the barrel, but more likely, he stood a chance of it literally backfiring and exploding in his face.

I did not punish him except that he had to suffer rather more than a one 'penny' lecture on his dangerous behaviour. In some ways, I blamed myself for this incident because he was bored and lacked the stimulation, which we should and would be giving the children in the future, but having been a home for younger children, we had very little equipment and materials for older children. Also, we were very busy re-organising things. However, Barnardo's was very helpful in getting us the necessary equipment or agreeing for us to make local purchases. The children mainly occupied them-selves in the small wood at the side of the house. They enjoyed charging downhill along the drive on old bicycles, which did not have any tyres or brakes. And, of course, the older ones missed the ponies. It was a great shame that we could not keep the ponies and Eileen and I were not too popular as a result but we eventually won the children over when we were able to start some new activities.

We had plans to start youth hostelling with the children as well as engaging in the Duke of Edinburgh Award Scheme. For these activities, we desperately required some serviceable bicycles and the present collection, which had obviously been given to the home in the past, and would need a lot of work done before we could take them on the road. I gathered the children together and told them what I intended to do and said that in the meantime, whilst we repaired the bicycles, we would lock them up. To my dismay, within a day or two the children were back on the cycles, crashing them and undoing our repair work. I felt very disheartened but I realised that I had not yet gained their respect or trust. I gathered them together once more and told them that I really did mean what I said about getting the bicycles back on the road and I explained it was not a challenge to see who could force my padlock, but I had put a cheap padlock of my own on just to remind them not to use the bicycles while they were being repaired. By using my padlock I told them that I was saving money because I would not have to buy one out of Barnardo's money and so there would be more money to spend on more interesting things like games and sports equipment. I was very pleased when I found that they did not break into the cycle shed again.

November 5th came and the children had been getting more and more excited as the great day drew near. After tea that day, I heard a bit of a commotion and the sound of crying coming from one of the bedrooms. On investigation, I found nine-year-old Richard howling his head off in great distress and when I asked his house-mother, one of the established staff at Chilton Park, what was the trouble, I was told that Richard had been awkward and defiant at the tea table, and was being sent to bed early at six o'clock as a punishment.

I pointed out that being sent to bed on firework night was out of all proportion to his defiance. As the house-mother was due to go off duty shortly, I told her that I preferred staff, when possible, to see the punishments that they gave through, and not leave it to other staff. On that night, we wanted all the staff who were on duty with the children round the bonfire and could not spare one member of staff to mind Richard in the house. I suggested to the house-mother that unless she wanted to stay on duty for the evening, she found a more suitable and practical punishment, which she did. I did not approve of sending children to bed as a punishment in any case, but that matter would have to come up at a staff meeting for discussion in the future.

The Round Table members and their families arrived in good time. The gardener lit the bonfire and soon it was burning fiercely. Having prepared their firework display earlier in the afternoon, the Tablers soon had the firework display going well and we all had an enjoyable evening together. We had cleared the squash court and were able to have our refreshments there. We were to find out that the Round Table would give us a lot of support and help during the next ten years and we were most grateful to them.

When the children from Barnardo's homes left school and went to work, they were usually supervised by their social worker who would find work or training and accommodation for them. As I was living with the children, I would usually have a closer relationship with them than they had with their social worker and so it was decided that I would be the after-care worker, when appropriate, for the boys. Mickey was the first boy that I took on in this role. Mickey was the oldest of a family of five that we had in care at Chilton Park. As he had left school the previous July, his social worker had found him a job on a farm some 15 miles away and also arranged lodgings for him, which were within a 15-minute cycle ride. It was then agreed, as I was on the spot, I would be his after-care worker. I had to make regular contact with both the farmer and his landlady in order to keep things running fairly smoothly. Although Mickey was a big strong lad, he did find the work quite hard. On one occasion, he was given the job of tying up the tops of the sacks of potatoes that had just been harvested. All went well until at the end of the day, when the workers went to load the sacks on to the trailer – the sacks burst open. Unfortunately, Mickey's knots were not up to the required standard and he had to do some unpaid overtime to retrieve the situation!

One day the telephone rang and it was our boss, Miss Roots, asking me to consider admitting a 12-year-old boy, who had a fascination for setting things on fire. She was desperate to find a suitable placement for him. I said I would discuss the situation with Eileen and the senior staff. We decided that we would have to say no to this suggestion. We all felt that we were geared to work with adolescents with behaviour problems, but that to admit an arsonist would alter the whole milieu that we were trying to establish. We wanted to do activities that would stretch our adolescents and be able to trust and rely on them when they were out of our sight. Such an admission would need a much more supervised regime to the detriment of the other children. I contacted Miss Roots and explained that we did not feel that this was the right placement. However, not wanting to sound too negative, I said that I did not mind how many difficult adolescents she sent us, within reason. I realised that I had rather 'nailed my colours to the mast' but in the years to come we found working with adolescents immensely rewarding.

One of our more urgent problems that required attention was the fact that all the older children went to the same secondary school, travelling on the same school bus, a journey of about eight miles. As there were a total of 18 boys and girls from Barnardo's, it had several undesirable results. They used to fool around on the bus and we had several complaints from the bus owners with threats of banning the ringleaders. Also, they all grumbled about their school and did not take as much pride in their school as they would if they went to different schools. The local education authority insisted that they all went to the one school. The junior school children were less of a problem as they were fewer in number and it was only a short journey to their village school. We were able to get Anne into a nearby school, as we were willing to drive her there and back ourselves. It gave her a break from the children she lived with as well as getting our individual attention on the car journey. We decided that Eileen, with her teaching background, would pursue the problem of secondary schools after Christmas and endeavour to get the secondary age children to different schools in the future.

November soon passed by and our thoughts turned to Christmas. We explained to the childcare staff that they could either have leave at Christmas or could have it over the New Year in order to have sufficient cover of staff for the children. This was not good enough for one member who took her leave at Christmas and never returned! Another young assistant house-mother, a Dutch girl, was going on two weeks holiday at the end of November and before she went, I had a quiet word with her. I explained that we had made changes since Eileen and I had arrived but that she had tended to ignore them and continued as before. She explained that had I been there when she'd first arrived, 18 months previously, she would most likely have done things my way but she could not change now. I suggested that she gave the matter some thought while she was on leave and decided whether she wanted to do things my way or, if she wished, I would enquire within Barnardo's if there was a suitable vacancy in a younger children's home. She went on holiday to Holland and did not return.

There were two problems that made the changes we were making difficult for the original staff. Firstly, they had to get used to working with older children and this was more of a challenge to some, and also we had changed the ethos of the home and it was now more child orientated. Staff had to work longer hours and work with the children rather than put them to bed early and go off duty. The same applied to holidays, especially at such times as Christmas, when it was important for the staff to share some of their time with the children, which was why staff did not have the whole of Christmas and New Year off. Working with older children was very rewarding but also more demanding in many ways.

Good news! Through a contact with the Diocesan Youth Chaplain, we thought we had found a suitable resident cook. She would be coming down for an interview the next day, and she would be able to start in a few days' time, as she was not in employment. Milly was in her 20s and used to adolescents as her last job had been cooking in an Outward Bound adventure centre in Scotland. Milly was very keen to take the position of resident cook when she came for interview, and we were quite impressed and felt she would fit in with the other staff. Eileen was absolutely delighted that she would not have to be responsible for the Christmas dinner!

I found that there were a considerable number of books in the children's rooms and in order that they would be available for everyone to read when we had three groups I decided to start a library. It would be run like a normal lending library so that the children would get the idea of choosing a book, taking care of it and returning it when they had finished it. We were quite often given suitable books and so there was usually a constant change and increase of books. There was a large empty glass-fronted cabinet in the hall and this made an excellent home for the library. The library was a great success among all ages and I soon got some volunteers to run it at fixed opening times. I could see that we badly needed books for the older children, especially encyclopaedias and other books they could refer to for their homework.

Chapter 14

Our First Christmas at Chilton Park

Our immediate thoughts turned to Christmas, which was fast approaching, so all future plans would have to go on the back burner for the moment. The first reminder of Christmas was a telephone call from a gentleman who worked in the maintenance department of a large paper mill. He had recently lost his young daughter in a tragic accident, and his mates at work had collected a sizeable sum of money for him and he wished to spend this money on a charity. He wanted to know if we would be interested if he was to offer to hire a coach and take all the children to London for a day. The children would be given a party meal and then taken to see a pantomime. I said it sounded like a very generous offer and that I would like to discuss the idea with him, so I invited him to visit us, which he accepted.

After a discussion with Eileen, we decided that for the sake of one day's pleasure for the children, the money could be so much better spent if it was used to buy equipment for the older children for sports and leisure. I spoke to Miss Roots at headquarters and explained my dilemma – that there was a chance of upsetting Mr Manning if I didn't accept his offer on his terms. Miss Roots agreed that I should have a frank discussion with him and explain how the gift of equipment would give pleasure over the whole year and more, rather than only last a single day.

Mr Manning made an appointment to visit us and we explained

the situation. We showed him round the home and by the end of the visit, we had won him over to our suggestion. I told Mr Manning that I was very keen for the boys to be able to do woodwork and crafts but we had neither the tools nor the bench to do such activities. I also mentioned, as we were showing Mr Manning around, that we were trying to get the bicycles roadworthy so that the children could learn to cycle on the roads safely, go youth hostelling and perhaps gain the Duke of Edinburgh Award. Mr Manning was obviously quite impressed and said he would go back to his work mates and see what they could do.

As it got nearer to Christmas, we started to get numerous phone calls offering us toys and gifts, both new and second-hand, from schools and churches. Whilst many of the gifts were very generous and new or almost new, all the parcels had to be carefully unwrapped. This was because we occasionally found that a worn-out or broken toy had been carefully wrapped in Christmas paper and was not suitable as a gift; also, we needed to know what the present was before we allocated it to a boy or a girl. But all the wrapping paper was re-used, if possible. We used the wine cellars as a sorting place for the Christmas presents and the staff called it 'Father Christmas' Grotto'. Since Barnardo's, at this time, did not give us any allowance to purchase presents, we were entirely reliant on gifts from the public. Most of our donors were unaware that Chilton Park had changed to care for an older age range of children in the past few months. For instance, a doll was hardly suitable for a 16-year-old girl. However, the staff were exceedingly generous and helped to make up this deficiency themselves. Later, Barnardo's was to recognise this problem and allow us to spend a small amount on the adolescents at Christmas. We asked the children to write a letter asking Father Christmas for their favourite presents, but at the same time saying we could make no promises. We endeavoured to give each child at least one item on their list, and if this was not possible from donated gifts, then the staff would usually dip into their pockets. Whenever a member of staff could spare the time, they would usually go down to the cellar and do some sorting or wrapping of presents. It was quite cold work in the cellar, but it was away from prying eyes.

Before and after Christmas the children were invited to a number of parties given by local organisations. The first one was in the village hall of a nearby village and they invited the children each Christmas. It took me two journeys to get all the children to the party in the minibus. Eileen went with the first group and I went back for the second group. On arriving at the hall, I followed the children into the building and was ushered into the kitchen, where I was invited to sit down and was given a plate of sandwiches and a cup of tea. I was rather bemused by this treatment and had expected to be given a seat with Eileen and the children. The organiser then went in to the hall and told Eileen that they were looking after 'her man' in the kitchen!

We were kindly invited to a number of parties, which the children thoroughly enjoyed, but, quite naturally, they tended to rate the parties by the size of the present they received at the end! When Eileen took over the running of the home before I could join her, she had to acquaint herself with a rather complicated system of bookkeeping and so we agreed that she would continue to be responsible for the accounting. I would take over the correspondence, weekly returns to headquarters and thankyou letters, which included thanking individuals and organisations for gifts and donations etc. I was kept very busy on the typewriter around Christmas time thanking all these good people for their help and support. There was no doubt that without their support, the children would have had a rather less satisfying Christmas.

As Christmas Day drew near the children became more excited. We told them that three of the older boys from Barkingside would be joining us for Christmas. They were now out at work and would have the usual time off for the holiday. Steven, Charlie's older brother, would be coming, as well as Richard and Fred.

Four days before Christmas Day, we had a telephone call from Mr Manning saying that he had some gifts for us, including two bicycles. He said that he would like to bring them round one evening and asked if he could bring two work mates with him who had helped in the collection of the money so that they could see where the money was going. Two days later, Mr Manning arrived in a large van with his assistants. He had not only brought two bicycles but a woodwork bench of substantial proportions, which he explained had been made by his friends who were all in the maintenance department. The request for tools and a bench had obviously appealed to them and they had generously supplied a wonderful collection of carpentry tools, both new and second-hand.

We then showed the three gentlemen around the home and introduced them to the older boys and girls who would be using their gifts. Over a cup of tea, we explained that we wanted the children to take the cycling proficiency test and then be able to use the bicycles for youth hostelling. Mr Manning said that although it had been planned as a one-off gift, he would think about collecting money again, and present us with more bicycles next Christmas. In fact, Mr Manning supported us in this wonderful manner for the next five years that we were at Chilton Park. During this time, we were given two more bicycles, tents and rucksacks for those taking the Duke of Edinburgh Award, reference books for our library to assist the children with their homework, as well as various board games.

In no time at all it was Christmas Eve, and our three visiting 'old boys' had arrived. Milly seemed to have the culinary side of Christmas well under control and had mastered the Aga. She had help from our two house-craft students, Joan and Penny. These were young girls who had left school and wanted to work in childcare but were too young for the position of assistant house-mother. They assisted the domestic staff in their daily work and learnt the domestic side of childcare as well as assisting the childcare staff.

The children went to bed very excited, hanging up their pillowcases on the end of their beds with an air of expectancy. Eileen and I took those who had been confirmed to the local church for the midnight communion. On our return, we sat down in the kitchen with some of the staff and the older boys to mince pies and ginger wine while we waited for the children to settle down and, hopefully, be fast asleep. Richard volunteered to be Father Christmas and dressed up in our Father Christmas outfit. In order to simplify things, we had filled similar pillowcases with the gifts and labelled them with the recipient's name. As Richard was changing over

Heather's pillowcases, she seemed to half wake up and said that she was thirsty. We quickly gave Richard a glass of water, which he handed to Heather. Next morning, Heather was full of her night's experience that Father Christmas had given her a glass of water!

The children, like children all over the world, were awake early and were busily unpacking their 'stockings', and seemed satisfied with the results. Some of the children had a family, which might lavish presents on them, while others did not get any presents from relations and we tried to even things up for them. Barnardo's had an 'Uncle and Auntie Scheme' which allowed volunteers to be an uncle or auntie to an individual child on a long-term basis. Such people could make a tremendous difference to a child who would otherwise not have any close contacts with the outside world.

We decided to put up tables in the entrance hall so we could all have Christmas dinner together. I was able to invite my parents over for the day as they now lived in a nearby village. It was good for the children to have people of grandparent age who would relate with them. Dennis, who came with us from Barkingside, made quite a relationship with them and would cycle over to visit them and he valued the feeling of being an individual and not one of a crowd.

On Boxing Day Mary entertained us with some impromptu acting from some of the children. On New Year's Eve, we organised a party for the older ones of secondary school age. This was a great success and they particularly enjoyed 'Murder in the Dark'. This was the first of many enjoyable Christmases we had at Chilton Park.

Chapter 15

Time for Change

During the holidays, we had talked to the children about moving them into three groups and had explained the advantages. We carefully selected the groups, keeping brothers and sisters together where possible. We asked the children to come up with the name of their group and it was decided to name the groups after the names of trees. Auntie Mary was in charge of the Cedarwood group. Auntie Sheila, who had joined us in the New Year and was an experienced house-mother, was in charge of the Pinewood group. And Auntie Jean, also with a lot of experience, and another new arrival at Chilton Park, was in charge of the third group, Aspenwood.

Meanwhile, Miss Roots had agreed that we could have the dining room divided to make a staff room and a room for the Aspenwood group. Cedarwood would have the playroom by the front door, and Pinewood would have the present staff room, which was situated near the kitchen. Weekday lunch for the domestic and childcare staff was taken in the present staff room and was a very formal and austere occasion. The sewing matron and the cook seemed to preside over the meal and when an unsuitable remark was made, it seemed it was the custom to change the subject by referring to the state of health of the tulip tree! This was a lovely and somewhat rare tree situated just outside the house. We were only too pleased to have an excuse to make things less formal and change this room to a group room.

With the wonderful gift of the woodwork bench and the carpentry tools, we had to decide where we would put the bench. As we had already decided that the ballroom was unsuitable for use as a bedroom, we realised that it would make a splendid recreation room. We took down one of the very simple partitions quite easily, giving us an 'L' shaped room and a partitioned-off area that would be the hobbies room, which was just the place to put the bench and tools. I found a couple of sturdy tables for model making on and we now had space for crafts and similar activities. We then moved a 6-ft-long slate-bed billiard table from the entrance hall to the ballroom and this still gave us room to have a table tennis table in the ballroom.

I now had a place to do some carpentry jobs, which became necessary as we formed the groups. The boot room was usually a jumble of shoes, sandals and wellingtons and I decided to make some shoe racks for each group. Each rack would have 12 sections with a shelf for each item of footwear and so each group would be responsible for the tidiness of their own rack. They would have to be well made and durable. It was surprising how long this task took me and it was only by investing in an electric drill that had various attachments, and working for an hour or two before breakfast, that I was able to complete the project in a reasonable time. The days were not nearly long enough but Eileen and I were so full of enthusiasm for the work in hand that we hardly noticed how tired we were until we went to bed!

The local farmer whose cattle grazed the parkland kindly agreed to separate off with electric fencing an area that we could use to play football. Bill had been a professional football player and not only was he enthusiastic but it was great for the boys to have him playing with them. I played on the opposite side to Bill and I was a poor player in comparison so I had to work extremely hard to keep the score fairly level with a lot of help from Bill! We used to play on Saturday mornings and while it was intended to give the boys some fresh air and exercise, I felt quite shattered and only recovered after a good soak in the bath and a cold orange juice. It was during these soaks that I got some of my best ideas.

One idea I had was to have a monthly art competition, when the children were invited to submit as many paintings as they chose. These paintings were hung up on the wall in the ballroom, and at the end of each month, I chose the best painting from each of the three age ranges. These winning pictures remained on the wall until the end of the year when I would judge them and select the best painting in each group for the year. I gave some sweets to the younger winners each month and a small cash prize to the winners of the older category. At the end of each year, I gave paint boxes to the three winners as prizes in the competition. The staff found this painting competition was most helpful. When a child said they were bored and did not know what to do, the house-mother could suggest they painted a picture for the competition and the thought that it might be a masterpiece gave a little more incentive. The children got a thrill to see their picture hanging on the wall, especially if it was the painting of the month.

One day, Mr Green, the gardener, came to me and said he would like to order some seeds, and to his surprise I said I would like him to show me round the garden. He was not used to the superintendent being interested in the garden and I think he felt it was more like interference than interest. I was most interested in his work because I had originally trained in horticulture and I wanted to maximise his contribution to the establishment. I suggested that instead of the house-father mowing the lawns in front of the house each week, as was the present practice, I felt this was the gardener's job to do as well as looking after the flowerbeds. I wanted the house-father to spend his time with the children, not gardening!

Mr Green grew vegetables in the walled-in kitchen garden for the house and it was all hand cultivated. Outside the walled-in garden, the gardener had quite a large area where he grew potatoes each year. As he had to hand dig this area and did not rotate crops, it was only giving a fairly low yield for all the work entailed. I told him that he could reduce his potato growing if he found he hadn't time with the extra job of looking after the garden in front of the house. I said

I was going to have a croquet game for the children there and wanted the lawn kept in good condition. When I asked for a key to the walled in garden he told me that he held the only key. The gardener was clearly a law unto himself and did not like interference. I told him that I would get a key cut for myself. As time went by, Mr Green accepted that while I had made some changes to his work, I was not completely unsympathetic and he proved a loyal and hard worker.

It became my job to supervise the ballroom and all its activities. It was proving so popular that the children wanted to go up there all the time. I made up a small blackboard that stood in the front hall on which I announced either 'ballroom now open' or when it would be open that day. Unfortunately, the children were too impatient and sometimes, when I wrote up 'ballroom open 2.30pm' at ten 'o clock in the morning, they rushed straight up there and then wondered why it wasn't open! So I resorted to sometimes writing partly in pictures so that they had to read it more carefully. This worked out very well and they learned to be more careful with their reading. The ballroom was open at least once every day and usually twice during holidays and at weekends. We now had the billiard table in there and Bill had retrieved two table tennis tables from the squash court, which he renovated. Bill was an expert table tennis player and had visions of us having several teams playing in the local table tennis league next winter. He decided that one of the tables would be good enough to play on in the league. I left it to Bill to be responsible for table tennis coaching for the children and the staff. Bill said that we needed an adult to go with each team for the away matches and that it was important for the children to have an adult playing with them. It was brilliant the way some of the staff responded and were duly being coached for the next winter when the league matches would start.

We had gained a record player given by a kindly donor and this was installed in the ballroom. The older children wanted us to have a record club, where all members subscribed threepence a week and took it in turns to choose a record when enough money had accumulated. Once again all the staff joined in and it was very successful and I will never forget some of those tunes which were played almost non-stop at times when I was playing table tennis or working with the children in the hobbies room. They were very happy times. After all, it was the swinging sixties!

One day, whilst walking in the wood where the children played, I noticed lots of tiny bulb-like leaves coming up. On mentioning this at lunchtime, I was told by Miss Ashton that the leaves I had seen were snowdrops, which would soon cover the floor of the wood with a mass of white flowers. This reminded us that spring was fast approaching and we still had a lot to do before the Easter holidays.

We arranged with the local policeman that he would come and give instruction to the children in order that they could pass the cycling proficiency test. This was a prerequisite before Barnardo's would allow the children to ride a bicycle on a public road. Bill had been very busy behind the scenes repairing the old bicycles so that they were roadworthy and would be ready in time for the proficiency instruction. I think Bill found this a longer job than he had anticipated because the bicycles were in such a bad state before we 'rescued' them.

With a feeling of spring in the air, Charlie came up to me and asked if he could have a spot for a small garden plot. He remembered that I had obtained a spot for Arthur to have one at Barkingside. I sounded out the older children and got a good response from about ten of them that they would like to have a plot themselves. The next question was – where? I took Charlie with me on a tour of possible sites and we came to a decision that an area of rough grass in front of the house, which was railed off and contained an empty shallow padding pool, was the most suitable place.

The children started off with great enthusiasm, which was not dampened by a shortage of tools. I let them use my tools and scrounged a few from the gardener. I don't think he thought much would come of this odd craze! It was lovely to see the joy the children were getting from planning their own gardens, but I wondered how I could keep their interest up between the hard work of digging and the delay before seeing their seeds come up. After a lot of thought, I decided to mark the gardens once a month for neatness and quality of the produce. There would be an annual award for the best marks over the year. This announcement was made just as their efforts were beginning to flag and they attacked their gardens with renewed energy. I only hoped that their renewed enthusiasm would last until they had some visible reward of some seeds coming up.

Chapter 16

Easter and Summer 1962

The three boys that we had brought with us from Barkingside had already shown the children their model aeroplanes that they had made at the village. They were keen to continue their model making of aeroplanes and I thought that the best way to get the others interested would be to have a chuck glider competition that would last for just the Easter holidays. This way I would be able to introduce model plane making gradually to the children and the younger ones could also have a go. Indeed, I had to make one for Anne so that she could join in. The first glider they made was free, and after that they had to pay a nominal charge if they built a new one. There was no charge for materials for repair of an existing one. We had one flying session a day, out in the grounds, when either Bill or I would time their flights with a stopwatch. The longest flight of the holidays would win an aeroplane kit. We also had a mending session at the end of the day so that they were ready for flying the next day. I recorded their best flights on a chart so they could easily see how much they had improved.

We found that the glider flying was very popular and we continued with this each Easter holiday, but I discouraged any suggestion to do this more frequently so it came as a fresh activity at Easter. One year the competition was won by one of the girls, Betty, who was particularly good at throwing a cricket ball and this obviously helped.

When I asked her what she wanted as a prize, she immediately put me down by saying a model aeroplane kit! It was interesting that the girls often wanted to make things out of wood, but the boys were the ones who wanted to learn weaving.

A lady spoke to me on the telephone one afternoon and asked me if I would like a gift of three table weaving looms for the home. I readily accepted, thinking at least one of the house-mothers would know all about weaving and it was nice to have a new activity that I thought would be more girl orientated. To my surprise, none of the staff admitted to having a knowledge of weaving. There was only one answer – I would have to see if there were any courses in weaving available. I duly enrolled at Canterbury School of Art for a beginner's course in weaving on Wednesday afternoons. And so I was able to keep one step ahead of the boys, who wanted to learn to weave, as well as one or two of the girls who were also interested.

The lady who gave us the weaving looms was so pleased that we were making good use of the weaving looms that she offered to me as a personal gift a large floor-standing loom that she no longer had room for in her house. I replied, "It is far too valuable to give to me." She then said, "You can have it on an indefinite loan." I accepted the loom on those terms. I couldn't see the children being able to manage it without a lot of practice, but I was very keen to use it. Firstly, I had to make one or two missing parts, which was not too difficult. Using my newly acquired knowledge of weaving, I managed to weave a tie and then a length of Harris tweed. Then one day the lady got in touch with me and said she would like to have the loom back. I was disappointed, especially as I had spent some time repairing it, but I was truly grateful for the table looms she had given us and the children were really enjoying making table runners on them.

At the beginning of the Easter holidays, the local policeman came along to commence his course of instruction for the cycling proficiency tests. He decided that the best place to have the instruction would be on the tennis court. Ten children passed the course and were presented with their certificates and two of the younger ones were told to have a little more practice before they could be awarded their certificates. The successful cyclists were able to go for a short cycle ride the next day, supervised by Mary and Bill, to celebrate their success.

We also had to start preparing for summer activities. This included selecting a team for the inter-homes sports and all the practice that entailed. Bill had a friend who was the captain of the cricket team that had their ground just inside our park. Bill got permission from the cricket club that we could practise and play games on the cricket ground as well as flying our model aeroplanes there. The club manager said that whenever our gardener wanted a second pair of hands to help him, the groundsman of the cricket club would be pleased to help. He was quite a young lad and as he was employed full time, he was not very busy in the winter. In spite of all the parkland, there was not really anywhere to play outdoor games that required an area of level grass, and also the trees in the park were a threat to our model aeroplane flying.

In spite of a lot of practice, mainly organised by Bill, only four girls and one boy got through the area finals and into the finals at Barkingside. It was a strange feeling going back to Barkingside and stranger still not to be running the sports day. It was lovely to meet old friends in the village but there was not much time as we had to get back to Canterbury the same day. Mark managed to come third in the 400yd race, while Betty managed a fourth in the 200yd and Wendy had a fourth in the high jump. I think they did very well to get so far and we were proud of our small team. The children were slightly disappointed, especially Mark who was always inclined to be a trifle over confident and he did not want to practise for any event, believing that he was the best anyway.

Although it was our first summer at Chilton Park, we managed to produce both a rounders team and a cricket team and had a few games against other local children's homes with mixed results. Bill coached the cricket team and, as he was an all round sportsman, we were very fortunate to have him with us.

A well established summer event was the annual outing to Joss Bay, a small picturesque bay on the East Kent coast. A local fruit packing firm provided this treat for all the children and staff. They

94

provided a bus to take all of us to the bay and the three groups quickly established themselves on the sandy beach. Everyone then was given an ice cream after which bathing costumes were the order of the day. A football was produced and a game ensued between the older boys and our hosts. Those not playing football paddled in the sea or had a swim. We were so lucky with the weather, it promised to be a glorious day and apparently, we were told, they were usually lucky with the weather. No wonder the children looked forward to the Joss Bay outing so much. At lunchtime, we were provided with a tasty picnic lunch. While a few of the children had a rest the others wandered off to explore the rock pools as the tide receded and we made sure that a member of staff was always nearby where the children were playing. With 30 children and about ten members of staff, it would be very easy for a child to slip away out of sight from the staff for a moment and then be in some sort of trouble. I am glad to say that all went very well and after a picnic tea, we boarded the coach once again for a final treat, more so for the older ones I think. On the way home we visited the firm's packing sheds and refrigerated stores. The children loved walking into the freezing cold stores on such a hot summer's day, and tasting or sucking the frozen hard blackcurrants. They certainly never tired of the Joss Bay outing and I know Anne enjoyed it very much and would never miss going while we were at Chilton Park.

Our last event of the summer was a holiday for all the children at Eastbourne. We had decided to go to Eastbourne again where we knew the facilities and it was a complete change for most of the children. We had arranged to use the same church hall only we were 30 instead of 12 children and ten staff instead of four. It was a bit of a squeeze with little privacy. The girls and ladies shared the stage, with the curtains drawn! The men and boys slept in the main hall. We used old mattresses to sleep on and used the usual facilities of such a church hall for washing. There were plenty of tables and chairs for meal times and we found enough crockery and cutlery for our needs.

We were lucky with the weather and the children spent most of the days on the beach or in the sea. The three groups made up their own sandwiches for their lunch and we all joined in a cooked high tea. After tea, Eileen and I took the older ones for a walk along the front while the groups got the younger ones ready for bed. A few turns on the slot machines on the pier was a very popular choice on the walk. If we had a wet day, we came well prepared as we had brought a supply of board games to suit all ages. The games of Monopoly and Risk were very popular, as were card games. The groups found the main swimming pool and then they found one further from the sea but much cheaper.

All too soon, it was time to pack up and return to Canterbury after a holiday enjoyed by everyone in spite of the rather limited accommodation. Whilst we enjoyed Eastbourne very much we did feel we must look into something a little more comfortable.

Chapter 17

Autumn and Winter Activities

No sooner had we unpacked from our Eastbourne holiday than we found we were getting the children ready to start the new school year. As Eileen had been a school teacher, she had been tackling the local education authority since the beginning of the year, with a view to allowing us to place some secondary school age children in any of the local schools in Canterbury and district. At the present time, all the children of secondary school age had to attend one rural secondary school the other side of Canterbury. We had already had a problem of bad behaviour on the school bus and because of the numbers they tended to get treated at school as a group and not individually. Since they all lived together, they never had the chance to be on their own but always part of a Barnardo's group.

We had obtained permission during the summer to send some children to the other local schools and we had bought the necessary school uniform for them. Soon after they had all started back at their schools, we became aware of another benefit from the change. Instead of grumbling about their school, they compared notes and spoke about the good points and thus had a much more positive attitude towards their school. We were able to make use of two schools in Canterbury and Bill would take the children attending these schools into the city in the minibus. I would back up Bill on his days off and holidays. It was an extra commitment but well worth the trouble.

Once the children were back at school it was the time to start our indoor interests with the children. Number one with the boys was to start building model aeroplanes after having seen the ones made by Charlie, Dennis and Jimmy. They had saved up some pocket money during the summer and now I had promised them that on Saturday we would visit the model shop in Canterbury and they could buy their kits. There was a good deal of discussion beforehand regarding the type of plane they wanted to build. I think they were all rather over-ambitious and over-confident and not aware of their limitations. I had promised Steve, one of the older boys who was very painstaking with his modelling, that he could use a small model aeroplane petrol engine that I possessed. He chose to build a control line plane, which was controlled by flying it on the end of two strings attached to a simple handle. This gave control of the elevators, up or down. The rest of the boys chose reasonably straightforward kits but there was an overriding ambition to build the biggest one. I couldn't keep the boys away from the hobbies room for the rest of the term.

Dennis was the boy who had been most keen on building the model railway at Barkingside, and he was most disappointed when we moved that I left the railway behind, because the other boys would have missed it very much. However, I had promised Dennis that when we moved to Canterbury we would have plenty of space to build an even larger one. Dennis now took me to task and asked me where the model railway would be built and when he could start. I would have to fund the model railway and as I supplied the boys who were making model aeroplanes with glue and all other materials to complete the model once they had bought the kit with their own money, I could see that life was getting a trifle expensive. At least I enjoyed these activities and it was a great privilege to open the door for the children and see them enjoy new skills.

Once again thought had to be given to where we could build the railway. This time space was not a problem but we had to make a guess as to how much room it would need as it developed, without taking up unnecessary space. The obvious place would be just inside the ballroom in line with the hobbies room partition wall. It would be close to workshop facilities and would have an area of about 10x20ft, without protruding into the activity area of the rest of the room. I agreed we could start building the baseboard and I sent Dennis off to see what materials he could find in the sheds where we parked the cars and kept the bicycles. I also suggested that he looked at the discarded furniture in the squash court. We would have to draw up some rough plans so that we knew where we had to put the woodwork in order to support the track. After my apprenticeship, courtesy of the local model shop in London, I now felt quite confident of knowing what was required. This time I had three experienced assistants.

Running all these activities took a lot of my time and so I hit on the idea of the older children being more involved in supervising some of the activities, which would give them a sense of responsibility. In the stamp club, I had encouraged the children to collect a limited number of countries or collect a theme or themes. For instance, Anne was already collecting stamps with fish depicted on them. I encouraged the children to arrange their stamps neatly and if possible in loose-leaf albums. I got all my friends to collect used postage stamps for the club but we did not get enough variety that way, and so I bought stamps at the local shop and then sold them at half price at the club meeting. I found they didn't value the stamps they got free so I charged a nominal amount for the stamps my friends gave to me. This 'profit' helped to pay the cost of selling the stamps from the shop at half price. Sometimes we would have a swapping session or auction off their spare stamps.

All these activities in the club gave an opportunity to appoint a secretary, treasurer and an auctioneer etc. They loved to have a title and enjoyed the responsibility it entailed. I suggested that they formed a junior stamp club, to be run by the committee members of the senior stamp club. This was a popular idea and the juniors enjoyed having their own club.

I had promised Bill that we, the staff, would practise our table tennis during the summer and so let him enter a team with the children in the local table tennis league. Eileen and Sheila agreed to play in the league as well as myself. I think Bill's enthusiasm to get us playing in the table tennis league blinded his judgement of our skill. We entered two teams under Bill's persuasion. Eileen and Sheila would take it in turns to play in the 'A' team with two of the children and I would play in a boys' team. Bill explained that we could register as many as we liked in a team but no one could be registered for two teams. We all practised hard for the first weekly match. There was great enthusiasm combined with not a little optimism. The 'A' team played the first night and it was unmitigated disaster! The team lost very easily 9-0. Eileen played that night and felt the standard, even in the lowest division, was too high for us. My team played later that week and we were beaten 7-2. I won a game and Mark, who was the best natural player among the children, managed to win a hard-fought game.

The idea of having staff playing in the team was not only to look after them and drive the team to the venue, but also to support the children when things went badly. Unfortunately, I detected a lowering of moral with the two ladies as well. I was very disappointed but I had to persuade Bill, somewhat reluctantly, to withdraw the 'A' team from the league by Christmas. My 'B' team survived that first year and we ended the season second from bottom place, which was really more than we had expected at the beginning of the season. We had several close matches but our inexperience showed up. However, the important thing was that the children had enjoyed the experience and were not down hearted, and had vowed to practise hard for the next season.

We all agreed that we had been too hasty putting the second team in at this stage, but Bill had a friend called Monty and he had begun to take an interest in our table tennis teams and after Christmas, he started coming over to coach the children. Anne was proving to be very good at table tennis for her age and was very keen. Eileen resorted to teaching and encouraging new children to the home, to learn to play.

As autumn approached, Eileen and I decided we would like to have a dog and we knew that this would be a popular decision with the children, particularly with Anne. We felt that the children were a bit vulnerable playing in the woods and there was a right of way pathway at the side of the house, which was open to the public. We also had a lady who came from another village in her car to exercise her dogs along the right of way. She claimed she had permission from the previous superintendent but when one her dogs bit one of the children, I told her that she must exercise her dogs elsewhere. Fortunately, it was only a slight bite, but it was a frightening experience for the little girl.

We decided after a lot of thought to have a Great Dane. This was partly because we'd had one ourselves before, but we also felt a large dog like a Dane would be more tolerant of the children. Its size would discourage children from teasing it, and not least, discourage unwanted visitors. I had found a breeder in Sussex who had puppies for sale and arranged to go down to choose a puppy. One Saturday we took the minibus and offered seats to the children to come along and help us choose. We filled up the seats in the minibus without any hesitation from the children. We thought it was nice to involve the children with choosing and naming the new pet, as they would in a normal family.

By the time we had returned to Chilton Park, the children had already named the new puppy. After a lot of discussion, they decided we would call him Kim. As soon as we had returned home he was introduced to Fugi, the cat, who was so named as it was short for refugee. She merely arched her back and hissed at Kim. He soon settled down and slept in the office at night until one morning we could not open the door to the office. Kim had got a trifle bored when he woke up that morning and decided to lift up the linoleum covering the floor, starting by the door. Perhaps he thought he should have a carpet!

We soon realised that we would need somewhere to put Kim when we were out or busy and ensure that he did not get in the way. We solved this by putting up a fairly large enclosure of 5ft-high chain link fencing with a small shed that had two doors, one giving access to the shed and the second one from the shed to the enclosure. A couple of years later, when Kim had grown to full size and we were both going out, I put Kim into his pen. It was just a day or two before Christmas and the staff were rather busy preparing for the festive season. One of our old boys from Barkingside days, named Fred, had joined us for Christmas and he thought he would go into Kim's pen to stroke him. Unfortunately, Kim did not know Fred and whilst he let Fred in, he would not let him get near the door to get out. Fred had to wait until we got back. Kim did not harm Fred in any way. He just would not let him escape.

As we got to the middle of October, I was reminded that Bill, Mary and I had completed a year at Chilton Park. Time had gone so quickly and we had achieved such a lot. But there was still more to do than we ever would dream about, but that is another story.

At the end of October one of our group leaders, Mary, announced at staff lunchtime that 31st October was Halloween and she suggested that the groups had a Halloween party. This involved the staff cooking some rather weird looking dishes that tasted slightly better than they looked, and some of the children dressing up as witches. I suggested that I took pictures of the three parties with my cine camera. The film was only 8mm wide and cost 30 shillings for four minutes of film, which, of course, could only be used once. This was quite expensive in those days and I could only allocate one film to the three groups. The children were quite excited and loved seeing themselves over and over again on the 'silver screen'.

The next highlight for them was November 5th when, once again, the Round Table came out to give us their usual spectacular display. This time, after the usual hot drinks and sandwiches, the boys took our visitors upstairs to the ballroom and proudly showed them the model railway. It was in its early stages, but they were able to operate an engine. This became an annual event after the firework display. We tried to make the most of national events, particularly sporting events, to both stimulate the children and make them more aware of the world outside Chilton Park. We used to make as much fun for the children as we could by Eileen and I supporting different sides when we watched a contest or a match. This resulted in a lot of friendly banter between us as well as showing the children that you could have different views on things without having to fall out with each other.

For our second Christmas, we decided to repeat the pattern of the previous year and we all had our Christmas dinner together in the entrance hall. Each of the groups decided to put on a mini pantomime to entertain us all. This was performed in the ballroom on Boxing Day. This year two of our old boys, who had just joined the army and were with us for Christmas on leave, spent a lot of the holiday period playing 'soldiers' with the younger boys. The boys were thrilled to bits to be playing with real soldiers and it was so nice to see the old boys 'let their hair down' and amuse the younger boys, even if it was a bit noisy. There were constant shouts of "bang, bang – you're dead" – "Oh no I am not" all round the house.

Chapter 18

1963 – Consolidation
and the Tale of Two Cakes

Eileen and I had been together at the helm for about 18 months and we now felt we had begun to establish a pattern for the general running of the home, giving a sense of security for the children. We had a happy and hard working group of staff, all of whom pulled together. The senior staff had all been together for over a year. We had weekly staff meetings and tried to involve all the staff in decision-making.

However, naturally it was not all honey. We were dealing with disturbed children who had been moved from their own home for various reasons. Some were with us because of fostering breakdowns and such breakdowns inevitably gave the child a sense of failure and inadequacy and needed sensitive handling. Some of the children we admitted were difficult adolescents who had caused problems in other children's homes. We loved them all but not always their behaviour! It was important for the child to have a good relationship with at least one member of staff with whom they felt they could confide. The younger children naturally tended to relate best of all with the staff in their group, while the teenagers might often form a relationship with Eileen or myself. We presented the children with the opportunities to follow a considerable choice of hobbies and activities. This did help to keep them occupied but this was not the main reason. Helping a youngster with a hobby enabled you to have individual time with the teenager. It gave them confidence, which was so important when they were mixing with their peers in the world outside the home.

These activities gave them an incite into a world of which they might never have had any knowledge. One boy carried on with his stamp collecting after he left us and he went out to work. He had specialised in the stamps of Great Britain and had increased his knowledge to the extent of playing the dealers at their own game! He would buy stamps from one dealer and sell them to another dealer, making a profit. He then hired a regular 'pitch' in an indoor market to sell stamps in his spare time. When the opportunity arose, he bought the indoor market and gave up his job. He now runs the market and with the help of his son has his own stall there as well. He has more recently bought adjoining property as well as converting the floor above as student accommodation.

As we came to the end of March and the end of the table tennis league games, Bill's friend, Monty, offered to run a table tennis tournament for the children and staff one weekend. There would be two age groups for boys and also for girls and one for the staff, as well as a doubles tournament. Monty supplied cups as prizes and the children played with great enthusiasm in the ballroom. We had played our league games in the squash court as the floor and lighting was ideal for table tennis. Unfortunately, it was unheated which made it rather chilly for spectators and we had to place black painted screens at each end of the table because the walls were painted white. Steve was the overall champion of the event. This tournament was most enjoyable, thanks to Monty, and was to become an annual event, which Monty organised each year and supplied all of the prizes.

We had decided that we would only have the glider competition during the Easter holidays so that it would come as a fresh activity each year. Of course, they could build a chuck glider any time but there would only be an organised competition at Easter. Our main Easter activity would be youth hostelling, which would give the older children a sense of adventure and achievement, a taste of the out-door life and a chance to meet people outside of Barnardo's.

Bill took three of the boys cycling for four days along the south coast and seven of the older girls with two assistant house-mothers did a five-day walk. I drove the walking party in the minibus as far as Reigate in order that they should not have too strenuous a walk to their first youth hostel. It was an ordinary April day when I dropped them but I did notice a slight chill in the air. After I had travelled about five miles on my return journey, it started to snow and I felt concern for the walking party on their first youth hostel trip. The road surface looked fairly good until the minibus slid a bit as I slowed down behind another car. I then stopped to give a lift to a driver whose car had gone into the ditch. In spite of my caution, the minibus slid to the right and when I attempted to correct it, the vehicle slid off the road onto the grass verge. Fortunately, we did not go in the ditch, and I was able to get back on the road.

Two narrow escapes within half an hour was too much for my passenger and he decided to walk was the safer option. About half a mile later, driving extremely cautiously, I came to a long hill with stationary nose-to-tail vehicles all the way up the hill. It appeared a sudden cold change in the air temperature had frozen the melting snow to a sheet of ice and the cars could not get up the hill and I had to wait patiently for nearly two hours before the road became passable. Unfortunately, I had not brought an overcoat and whilst I had reasonable fuel for the journey, I did not like to run short as I might if I kept the engine running in order for the heater to operate. I was very glad to get home and was relieved to hear that the children had reached their youth hostel safely. The boys returned safely under Bill's care and had a lot to say about their adventures, and the next day the girls returned proudly talking of their achievements. To sum up, we could truly say everyone had enjoyed it and was looking forward to the next trip.

As soon as the children were back at school for the summer term, we had to prepare for our summer fete. Apparently, the money raising side of Barnardo's in the Kent area was represented by Tom Smith and he expected us to have an annual fete on the Saturday of the May bank holiday. We had been let off having one last year as we were just settling in. We had a tremendous lot of help from the Barnardo's Helpers League organised by Tom Smith, the local Scouts who organised an aerial ride on a rope, and the Round Table, who ran some of the side shows. I painted a target with a central hole to aim a football through. And I also painted a background on a board of a man in the stocks for people to throw wet sponges at the person's face looking through the central hole. When I took my turn as a volunteer target, the children thought it was pocket money well spent on throwing wet sponges at me.

We had a team of morris dancers performing on the lawn and a live steam model railway giving rides for the children. For me, the worst part was giving an opening speech of welcome to everyone and introducing the celebrity who would then officially open the proceedings. I was surprised to find that none of the children resented the fete in any way, such as feeling it was an invasion of their privacy. On the contrary, they felt it was quite natural to have an annual fete. After all, their school and the local church had a fete – why shouldn't Chilton Park have one? The day had been sunny throughout, and everyone appeared to have enjoyed themselves and Tom reported that the profits had been very good.

Future annual fetes followed a very similar pattern and the weather never seemed to let us down. Bill volunteered to make the opening speech one year, much to my delight, but he froze at the crucial moment and his words would not come out. The poor man felt so embarrassed, and I had to quickly take over. I quite understood his plight and it could well have been myself. The next year we were lent a 'Dalek' by the BBC and we were also lent a mechanical elephant giving rides, called Barney, which amused the children – Barney being my nickname that all my family know me by.

At the Canterbury army barracks' annual fete the first prize for the raffle was a cake model of Canterbury Cathedral. It was well made but quite large and the winner decided to give it to charity. The officer in charge and the cook who made it came out to Chilton Park and made a formal presentation of it to the home. Unfortunately, by the time we received the cake, it had become a little bit stale and when we cut it open, to the children's disappointment the cake was a little mouldy and the icing had gone very hard. It had taken too long to reach us and no doubt it would have been very nice had it been eaten within a short time of its making.

Some six weeks later, we were presented with another cake. A well-known firm of caterers and producer of fine cakes was entering a large cake in a British industrial fair fortnight in Zurich, Switzerland. This cake was so large that it occupied the best part of an entire low loader trailer behind a lorry. It was called the world's largest travelling cake. This cake was en route to Dover where it would cross the channel and as it passed through a town or a city, a small replica would be presented to the Mayor or, as in our case, the Sheriff of Canterbury. Being a local charity, the sheriff kindly gave it to the home and made a formal visit and presentation. However, there was a snag as the driver of the truck wisely decided that he could not get the truck up the half-mile long drive at Chilton Park. Consequently, we all had to go down to the end of the drive where we admired the giant cake. We then went back to the house for the formal presentation of the replica, which, I am glad to record, was more manageable in size. After the sheriff presented it to me, the cake was cut and a little voice was clearly heard to say, "I hope it is not mouldy like the last one." I recognised the voice – it was my daughter's!

Choosing a book at the library

Croquet

At work in the hobbies room

Ready to fly chuck gliders

Getting to know you - Kim and Fugi

Launching the mirror dinghy

Beach hut near Tankerton Bay Sailing Club

Chapter 19

Lee Abbey and Bad News

We had known of the Lee Abbey conference, retreat and holiday centre in North Devon for some time. It had an interdenominational staff and when we heard that they were holding a youth camp in August, we applied for details. We spoke to Miss Roots about taking some of our older boys and girls for a week to the youth camp. Eileen and I would pay our own expenses and book in with Anne to the house group. We would need to take the minibus to fit everyone in with our luggage.

Miss Roots suggested that we might like to include Sheila, a 16-year-old girl from a foster home, whom she felt would benefit a lot by joining our group. We were asked to take Reg, whom we knew, as he was the younger brother of Tony, one of our Barkingside boys. We also took Fred and Richard, from Barkingside days. From our present home we took Tom, Maria, Cathleen and Joan, the latter being one of our house-craft students.

We planned to travel through the night for several reasons. Firstly, some of the working age youngsters would have to work on Friday and actually started their holiday on the Saturday, the day the camp began. It was a long drive and the roads would be less crowded at night. It was the height of the holiday season and a lot of the holiday traffic funnelled into Devon via the notorious Honiton by-pass just before reaching Exeter. Fortunately, we would be going to North

Devon and traffic should be a little easier. I hoped my passengers might be able to indulge in a little sleep on the way as it would also be a boring journey and not all that comfortable. Eleven of us had to fit in a 12-seater vehicle in which we had to squeeze our luggage as well.

We also had a logistical problem. There were not very many petrol stations open 24 hours a day en route, and our minibus was not only quite thirsty but it would be fully loaded and it only had a small petrol tank. In the end, Eileen had a bright idea – ask the AA! The Automobile Association, of which I was a member, were most helpful. They gave me a route to North Devon, which encompassed filling stations that would be open 24 hours a day at suitable intervals. The first stop they suggested would be at Godstone, where there was an all-night garage on our route, the A25.

Milly, the cook, had produced a mountain of sandwiches for us and lemonade, and some flasks of tea. The minibus, which was quite old, had been checked by the garage, and was now filled to the brim with petrol. Anne had been to bed, in spite of her protests, to have some rest before the journey. The four young people from Chilton Park had been excited all day and now, as the remainder of the party assembled, the excitement increased. It was after seven o'clock that we finally got away, driving into the setting sun.

I knew that I was in for a lengthy and tiring drive, but we were not in any hurry as we had all night and the best part of Saturday, if needs be, to complete the journey before we would be late. The going got more difficult once we had to use our lights and then, just as we began to look for the filling station at Godstone, it appeared on our offside. I think all of us felt the sense of adventure and it was reassuring that the first item on the trip worked according to plan. Soon traffic began to thin out and driving got easier. Eileen managed to keep awake, checking our progress on the map, and making sure I took the correct turnings. After several hours of driving, we stopped at an all-night lorry drivers' café where we had a refreshment break as well as a chance to stretch our legs. We made several more stops, at decreasing intervals, as we got more tired or stiff, and were very grateful to Milly for our sandwiches and drinks.

Fortunately, we arrived safely without any incidents at about seven o'clock in the morning. I was so tired that I could hardly keep my eyes open but I managed to find a grassy car park near a shop just a mile or two away from our destination. The toilets in the car park were very popular. Some of our passengers found the journey much longer than they had anticipated and wondered if we would ever get to our destination. I told them that Lee Abbey was only a couple of miles away and as it was still early the morning, we could hardly expect a welcome. I was going to have a nap and I suggested that if they could not curb their impatience with a doze in the Bedford, then they could explore the village. The youngsters found it rather strange to be up and about and the shops were not open yet.

At half past eight, I suggested that it was time to complete the final part of our journey. Having unloaded our passengers and their luggage and directing them to the camp, we drove round to the main building where the three of us were staying with the house party.

We didn't see much of the boys and girls during the week as they had their own programme. In the house party we had an enjoyable time, which was memorable for me, for the completion of two long organised walks on Exmoor of 18 and 22 miles. Eileen and Anne enjoyed the shorter organised walks of two or three miles with a cream tea at the end!

All too soon, it was time to return home at the end of the week. In a slightly less excited manner, we made the journey home. By all accounts, the group had thoroughly enjoyed the camp and appeared to have taken in some of the Christian message that was given during the week by the leaders. They all summed it up in that they would go again if they had the opportunity.

Before the end of the summer holidays, we had a croquet tournament, which was won by Steve and Jimmy. Only a few weeks later Jimmy would be leaving us because he had eagerly accepted the opportunity offered by Barnardo's to emigrate to Australia. He was the only child we had in our care to go to Australia. He had no ties here and we trust that he settled well, but sadly, we did not hear how he got on after the first year or two.

An old school friend and best man at our wedding, Matt, had now been coming down from London regularly and became an 'uncle' to the children. They loved Uncle Matt and he was very popular, especially as he drove a fast sports car, which he was always changing for the latest model. He gave all the children ten shillings for their birthday present. Matt kept in touch with those working boys who had been with us at Barkingside and worked in London. He organised a short 'rag concert', which was performed by the working boys and girls who came back at Christmas. This consisted of a few hilarious sketches often taking the mickey out of me as the wicked uncle!

Christmas 1963 saw the three groups produce some outstanding entertainment, having gone to a lot of trouble and it showed that a little healthy competition did not do anyone any harm. Aspenwood, Auntie Jean's group, presented the dolls' 'tea party'. The children dressed up as the various dolls. Auntie Sheila's group, Pinewood, performed a traditional pantomime, and Auntie Maureen's group just dressed up and did sketches.

In March 1964, we had our annual table tennis tournament, organised once again by Monty, who as usual supplied all the prizes. The seven prize-winners included Mark who, with Monty's coaching, was coming along very well. The next year he was invited to play in the under-14 boy's team for the Canterbury league against other similar teams in Kent. His worst enemy was frustration and when things were not going his way, he had a habit of hitting his thigh with his bat. One day, when Eileen was watching, and he was not doing too well, and was banging his bat against his leg, Eileen called out to him to take care or he would break his bat. Two slaps later and he broke his bat! It was a lesson learnt, but a hard one. Table tennis bats were quite an expensive item for Mark to purchase out of his pocket money.

One day in March, the gardener said he was finding difficulty when shovelling the coke off the boiler room floor because the bricks were becoming loose and the shovel caught on the bricks. He suggested that if I could get him the sand and the cement he would concrete the floor, with the help of the young groundsman from the nearby cricket ground. I fully agreed and telephoned the works department at Barnardo's to seek permission to purchase locally the necessary materials. Much to my surprise, they would not give agreement but said someone would come down and check out the problem.

Two weeks later, Mr Wood came down from headquarters and examined the problem. To my utter surprise, Mr Wood said that he could not sanction my request as he was only authorised to agree to emergency repairs as Chilton Park was to be closed. I was completely stunned by this information and so was Eileen. We had carefully built up a good hardworking and caring staff team and had offered stability for the children for the last three years and now I was told the home was going to close. Where were the children going and had we lost our jobs? Most important, why were we not told about this before?

I was still rather angry, to say the least, when I got on the telephone the next day and spoke to Miss Roots. She was very apologetic and said that she had planned to come down and talk about it and deeply regretted that we were informed about future plans in this way. Miss Roots did come down and explain the situation. It appeared that it was thought that Chilton Park was rather out of the way for older children to be able to come and go freely as they took part in such events as after-school activities, Scouts or Guides etc. We fully agreed with this and had said so ever since we had been able to use the schools in the city. The idea, Miss Roots said, was to find suitable accommodation within the city of Canterbury, which might even be a purpose-built building. She said that we were not in danger of losing our jobs, and the children and staff would all be moving together. In any case, it was not envisaged that we would be moving for at least another two years. We let the staff know of the future plans at staff meeting, but agreed we would not inform the children until we had more certain information.

Chapter 20

1964 – Good News and a Wedding

In spite of the uncertainty of the future, life at Chilton Park had to go on, and the model railway was no exception. The track was all laid down and connected to the 12-volt transformer and the children were busy making plastic models of the buildings. It was time to lay down some guidelines so that the children could get the best out of the railway.

Talking to the older children who were interested in the model railway, we decided to form a model railway club limited to six members who would take responsibility for the efficient operation of the railway as well as taking a leading role in making the models. Each member would have responsibility for the regular maintenance of one of the locomotives. No one could operate the railway unless I, or a member of the club, was in charge. The person responsible would then enter their name in a book for the period they were in charge, noting any repairs required. We had acquired an old alarm clock that had been converted to run at the rate of an hour in five minutes, and trains ran to a simple timetable. Any child could operate the model, providing they could tell the time to the nearest quarter of an hour and a club member was present. This gave the young ones an incentive to learn to tell the time. It was important to run the railway to a timetable or else it would have involved racing and crashing trains. Because the children had been building it themselves, they took care of it, whereas if it had been given to us complete, I am fairly sure that after the novelty had worn off, it would gradually be destroyed by misuse. We could run six trains at the same time, or by switching over, we could run a simple timetable of two trains at once for the younger children's benefit.

Partly because I did not have unlimited funds to spend on the railway, we made a rule that we would only purchase ready-made locomotives and track. We would, if possible, make all the rolling stock and buildings from kits or, better still, from scratch. We sifted and dyed sawdust in various colours to represent grass and leaves on trees or ploughed fields. We used quite a lot of balsa wood and printed brick and tile paper purchased from the local model shop in Canterbury.

Occasionally, we would be given some second-hand model railway 'bits and pieces' which were most acceptable. Once we were given two Hornby Dublo locomotives, but unfortunately, they required 'three rail' track to run on and our layout used the more modern 'two rail' system. The engines were too good not to use them and I sent them away to a firm that specialised in converting them to two-rail operation. When I received them back from being converted, I was informed that there would not be any charge as we were a Dr Barnardo's home. I was most grateful to the firm and very much appreciated their kindness.

The children took great pride in their model railway as well as having a lot of fun operating it, especially for the benefit of visitors. Mr Manning continued to collect money at the paper mill and arrived just before Christmas with some of his helpers and brought us presents of cycles and camping equipment for our Duke of Edinburgh Award Scheme. It became a tradition for the children to operate the railway for the visitors before they went home after being served coffee and mince pies.

Some of the children were still enjoying working for the Duke of Edinburgh Award and Charlie was now working for his silver award. His hobby section for the award was aero-modelling, but he still devoted some of his time to the railway. The six members of the railway club had various titles – such as builder, chief engineer and general manager – and one of the girls was personnel officer, a title that 'tickled her pink' and she was responsible for the painting and placing of the little figures from plastic kits. Graham made a wagon from a kit with my help and whenever he saw it running behind an engine he would warn the operator to take care because he had made that wagon.

A telephone call from Miss Roots' secretary booked an appointment for her to visit us the following Tuesday. On arrival, she greeted us with the good news that Barnardo's was looking at a site in Canterbury, just off St Thomas Hill, where they would build a new purpose-built Barnardo's home. If all went well it was proposed that the Canterbury School of Architecture would design the building. This was exciting news for all of us.

One weekend, Eileen and I took four of the older girls camping to Birchington, a small coastal resort between Canterbury and Margate. I had by now traded my faithful Austin A30 for a Hillman Minx estate car. We just had room for the four girls, two tents and ourselves. Anne was staying with her grandmother for the weekend. We took Pam, Sally, Doris and Sarah. The girls were delighted at being in a small group and getting away from the routine of Chilton Park. The camping site was open to the public and on arrival, in a burst of enthusiasm, Sally – remembering her guide camping days – offered to go and 'dig' the toilets. I explained that on this site there were toilets and washing facilities provided. The only camping that Sally had experienced had been with the guides. It showed how important it was that children in care should get the chance to experience the world beyond their doorstep. The weather was fine and the girls very much enjoyed the experience, sharing in the cooking and getting individual attention. A popular activity was bathing in the sea and sunbathing, as the weather remained fine for the weekend. The girls were reluctant to return to Chilton Park after what had been a happy weekend.

A local newspaper had decided to organise a 50-mile walk from Margate to Maidstone and the children wanted to take part. Richard, an 'old boy' from our Barkingside days, had previously completed the London to Brighton walk and offered to come down from London and take part and give us his advice and experience. This we readily accepted. As usual, the staff willingly supported the venture with enthusiasm and even wanted to take part themselves. We insisted that not only must the children have some hard practice, but they would have to complete a minimum distance of 15 miles, before they could enter.

All thoughts of other activities took second place in the minds of those hoping to take part in this venture. It was unusual to hear children asking to go for a walk at the weekends so that they could practice for their 15-mile qualifying walk. By the time limit for entries, we had ten older boys and girls, four members of staff and Richard taking part. The staff included Jean, Doris, Joan – now an assistant house-mother – Milly the cook, and Richard.

The great day for the walk, a Friday, finally arrived. As the start of the walk was at midnight, we told the walkers that after their tea they would have to go to bed for some rest before we got them up at ten o'clock. I have never known children go to bed early, so willingly! They were too excited to sleep but at least they had a rest. At ten o'clock, they were called and had a hot meal. Bill drove the minibus and Eileen and I took three walkers in our car. At Margate, it was as busy as though it was daytime. We saw the start of the walk and then Eileen and I returned home to have some sleep before we took over from Bill, who we had arranged would patrol up and down the road keeping an eye on our walkers. He had hot drinks, food and plasters on board and would take anyone in the minibus if they wanted to drop out.

With five adults on the walk, we hoped the children could find someone to walk at their pace. We expected Richard to complete the walk and we thought Milly might well manage to finish, as she had previously been a cook at an Outward Bound unit in Scotland. We thought most of the children would do well to manage 15 miles.

Back at Chilton Park, the alarm woke us at five o'clock. We hastily dressed in warm clothes, had a quick breakfast and were on the road by six o'clock. Bill had returned and we took over the minibus. Two of the girls had come back with Bill suffering from sore feet! We soon found our walkers, who had now passed through

Canterbury, and were on the road to Charing. They were glad of a rest and food and drink, but were doing really well. By nine o'clock, we began to have more of the younger ones retiring, but Billy, the youngest boy, was going really well up in the front of our walkers, with Milly. Unfortunately, Billy had to retire with exhaustion on the outskirts of Maidstone. Milly went on to complete the walk along with Richard, Joan and Charlie, and so one old boy, two members of staff and one of our boys completed the walk. The rest of our team dropped out having achieved 20 to 30 miles. I think everyone was quite proud of what they had achieved. After a hot meal and a good night's sleep, no one was the worst for their adventure by Sunday morning. On Monday, I am sure they enjoyed relating their adventures to their school friends.

In September, we had the first of several weddings involving our young people. Tony, who had been our oldest boy when we first went to Barkingside, had a girlfriend in the village named Helen, and now they were going to get married and they asked if they could have the marriage in our local church. Of course, we were not only delighted but excited at the prospect. They had been such a sensible young couple when we knew them in our Barkingside days. Tony now had a good job as a civil servant. The couple paid us some visits in order make arrangements for the great day and it was lovely to see them again.

The day of the wedding arrived and they looked such a handsome couple, and the bride looked so lovely in her wedding dress. Tony's brother, Reg, was best man and Anne was one of two bridesmaids. Anne was thrilled to be involved and the weather was as nice as could be expected on a September day.

The reception was held in the ballroom, an ideal setting, and all our children and staff were invited. When we heard that they were going to Majorca for their honeymoon, we were all very jealous! Eileen and I had never been abroad, and only one or two of our staff had been so fortunate.

After the excitement of the wedding, we soon found ourselves in a winter routine, and when Monty had his table tennis tournament at the end of February, we knew that spring was just around the corner. This time Monty had provided no less than eleven cups to be awarded to the winners. Thanks to the coaching from Bill and Monty, our table tennis team was now competitive in the league and I had a friend who offered to play in our team the next season. I was going to play with two 15-year-old lads from a Methodist youth club who were very keen to gain promotion but needed an older person in the team to drive them to the venues. In the case of these two teams, our reserves would come from the children, giving more children the chance to play.

Chapter 21

Hostels and Boats

It was spring 1965, and for the Easter holidays we had planned some youth hostelling trips again. This Easter it was my turn to take the boys youth hostelling on bicycles. We planned a route taking three days to reach Brighton via the coastal route and then another three days returning by an inland route. We started off on a wet Monday morning and when we reached the coast at Hythe, we were facing a cold north-west wind and it was raining more heavily. We decided to have a break and have some of our sandwiches and a hot drink from our thermos flasks. We could not find anywhere to get out of the rain to have our break and so we had it in the gents' toilets!

We continued our journey facing a freezing cold wind and rain as we crossed Romney Marsh. By now we were very cold and as we were wearing shorts our legs got so cold that the boys complained that their legs had gone numb with the cold! We then had a stop at a café for some hot food and drinks to warm us up. With all my concern for the physical welfare for the boys, I forgot to pay. I did not realise my omission until some five miles further on. I left the boys at a café that we had just passed, with a cup of tea, while I returned to the café to pay the bill. The boys were impressed with my honesty and one of those boys was to remind me of the incident 40 years later.

We reached our first youth hostel that evening, near Hastings, without further problems. The next day the sun came out and we had a very pleasant ride into Eastbourne. The following day was a gorgeous sunny day, the best yet, and we arrived in Brighton quite early so that we could enjoy the sights. After one night in Brighton, it was time to turn towards home riding along country roads. With two remaining hostels left to try out, we did not have any more incidents but we all agreed we had thoroughly enjoyed the trip.

While I had been away with the boys, a group of seven children had enjoyed a walking youth hostelling trip. This group had been taken by minibus to the Windsor area so that they could walk along by the river to their hostel. The children were accompanied by one of our staff, Brenda, and a student from a residential childcare course, who was on a placement with us at that time.

For a few years we had been sent many students for their practical placements. Tutors made sure that the student would be properly supervised and their needs would have priority and they would not be used as stop-gap temporary staff. They required a student to be supervised by a trained or an experienced member of staff. This person would be called a student supervisor and would be expected to devote at least a weekly session to discuss with their student their progress and their problems etc. They would be responsible for writing a report on the completion of the placement.

As I had attended the basic course and was having students from that course on practical placements, Eileen and I were invited to attend a student supervision course in London organised by the Home Office. Later on, we were invited to attend a similar course as assistant tutors.

In the early part of the year we were asked by the general secretary of Barnardo's, who lived in Whitstable, if we would like to have two sailing dinghies that had been given to Barnardo's. One was a Cadet dinghy, a class of boat about 12ft long, designed especially for children to sail. The other was quite an old Enterprise dinghy with cotton sails, just over 13ft long and could take a crew of two or three. I was thrilled with this offer as I loved sailing and had always planned to have my own boat. The general secretary said he would arrange for us to have a beach hut at Tankerton, near

Whitstable. There was a sailing club there called Tankerton Bay Sailing Club and he said they would look after us, as he knew the club well. The club did not have any premises so we would need a beach hut for changing in, and the boats would have to be kept on the shingle beach next to the sea wall.

I decided that now the time had come for me to realise a long-held ambition of mine – to build a boat. A small sailing dinghy had been launched by the Daily Mirror newspaper, which could be purchased in kit form for £60. A spinnaker and the necessary paint were extra. Much was my excitement and the children's curiosity when I unpacked an 11ft-long cardboard parcel. I intended to build the boat before the Easter holidays so that I could then concentrate on teaching the children to sail. The Cadet dinghy was rather small for an adult to squeeze inside and the Enterprise, though an excellent boat for capable sailors, was rather too tender (liable to capsize) for the children at this stage. However, the Mirror was an excellent boat that could take a crew of three, but two was more comfortable. It was unsinkable with built-in buoyancy tanks and made an excellent racing or cruising boat.

After discussion with the staff, we felt that the best place to build the boat would be in Pinewood group room. Seeing the boat gradually emerge would, I hoped, help to stimulate the children's interest. It would be helpful for me to be able to work indoors rather than out of the way in the garage. By getting up early and working on the boat in every free minute, with some help from the boys, I was able to build it in two weeks! It took me one further week to paint it as I had to let the paint dry thoroughly between coats. I decided to paint the boat yellow, my favourite colour.

The first time I sailed the boat was a moment I won't forget. A friend came with me and I was happily surprised that everything seemed to work and I was quite thrilled when I had returned to the spot from which I had started! I felt I was in control. I named the boat 'Sea Imp'.

We were able to have a beach hut in the front row near the boats, which Barnardo's had organised for us. This beach hut was a great asset to all the staff and children, as Tankerton was only eight miles away from Canterbury. Before the children could start learning to sail they had to be able to swim 25yds in the sea with their clothes on. Charlie and Dennis were able to pass this test easily, coming from Barkingside, where there was a swimming pool. Only two or three of the others were able to pass the test that summer, as well as Anne.

Now we had some children who had passed their swimming test, we were able to bring over our three boats and keep them on the beach. We had bought some lifejackets for the children to wear at all times when sailing and now I had to teach them how to rig a boat, and how to crew. I had a friend who could sail who offered to come over and help the children. This helped to speed up the teaching process as we could now have two boats on the water at the same time and there would be someone to help if the other boat got into difficulties or capsized. We used to practise our sailing at weekends when the club were racing as this would mean they had a rescue boat on the water and would gladly help us if needed.

I had managed to acquire a second-hand set of Terylene sails to replace our cotton sails on the Enterprise dinghy. We carefully mastered our sailing skills that summer without having any dramas and made full use of the beach hut. We started a tradition that on bank holidays we would go over to Tankerton before breakfast and I would take the youngsters for a walk while Eileen organised the cooking of fried eggs and bacon for breakfast. I will never forget the wonderful smell of eggs and bacon as we returned to the beach hut. After washing up, we would get the boats ready for sailing, weather permitting.

Another sailing tradition was to have a laying-up supper when we had finished the sailing season and put the boats away. We used to take all those who had sailed to a Chinese meal at the local restaurant in Canterbury. This was a most popular event and at the beginning of the sailing season, we used to have fish and chips in the beach hut as our fitting-out supper.

Whilst many of the older children wanted to join in with the sailing, they were prevented from doing so as they were unable to swim the necessary distance. The schools they attended did not have swimming pools and Canterbury did not have an indoor one. We decided to take them to Eastbourne again for the summer holiday, but this time we would stay in the Barnardo's home while that family were away elsewhere. We knew that there was a good swimming pool at Eastbourne. We would divide the children into groups of five children and a house-mother from their house group. Each group would have a mixed age range of children and I gave each child a swimming card. This card listed a series of swimming exercises leading up to the child actually swimming. I had been taught a method of teaching children to swim at my course in London and so had Mary and Bill.

The course was based on the mushroom float, floating vertically with arms outstretched with the feet only a few inches from the bottom of the pool. It gave the person confidence that they could float, and was proceeded by a series of simple exercises to help build up confidence. These exercises were listed on their swimming cards and when the child had achieved one, it was crossed off and counted a point towards the group. Children below secondary age won double points. At teatime each day, I read out the latest total scores of the groups and we made a competition of the progress of the six groups.

The exercises started off with putting their head under water, breathing out under water, walking a width, achieving a mushroom float and finally swimming a width and a length. This was most successful and by the end of the fortnight, thanks to the enthusiasm of the staff, 11 children learnt to swim, as well as one of the house-mothers. This meant that three more children could pass the test to be allowed in the sailing boats, but they would only have a few weeks of the sailing season left.

That autumn we had the good news that Barnardo's had acquired the site in Canterbury and were going ahead with all the necessary planning permission and hoped to start building after Christmas, and the building would be ready early in 1967. We would miss Chilton Park very much and it had been a happy home for us all. However, the move would be the best thing for the children in the long run.

I tend to remember the good things rather than the problem times but we did have some unhappy moments as one would expect in most families. One traumatic event for Eileen occurred when she had a disagreement with a rather disturbed 14-year-old boy who had a violent temper. This event occurred in the kitchen and the boy picked up a sharp knife and pursued Eileen round the kitchen table. The large table kept them well apart, and Bill, the deputy, heard a rumpus and came to Eileen's assistance and the boy put the knife down. Fortunately, it was uncommon to have such extreme violence in the home.

After the usual Halloween parties we had another party in the beginning of December, when we celebrated the 21st birthday of Milly, our cook. The girls put on their best frocks and the boys wore ties. Milly wanted to share her party with the older children and so her family came to the party and we all had a nice time together.

We had a tradition that one of the old boys would dress up and visit us as Father Christmas in the afternoon on Christmas Day. The older children would try to guess his name. One year Father Christmas walked up the drive and the older ones noticed that one of the old boys was missing and presumed he was Father Christmas. However, to their amazement, as they later watched Father Christmas walk back down the drive, there was the missing old boy also watching out of the window! By discreetly changing the robes during the afternoon, the lads had completely confused the children.

We used to take some of the older children to a church in Canterbury where they could mix with youngsters of their own age and get some stimulation from a slightly more modern form of worship in a modern church. The young curate used to come out to us once a week and take a Bible study group with the secondary aged children. That Christmas he offered to come out to us on Christmas Day and dress up as Father Christmas. The curate arrived secretly, dressed up as Father Christmas, went round to the front door and was let in. The children did not recognise him and nobody was missing. He was a great success and asked the children if they liked their presents. He was given a drink, and amused everyone by insisting on drinking it through a straw to avoid getting his beard wet. No one guessed who Father Christmas was.

Christmas was over and we turned our thoughts to the New Year. It seemed likely that we would have one more Christmas in this lovely old house, but how wrong we were to be!!

Chapter 22

The Final Year

Nineteen-sixty-six started off with a heavy snow fall and the children were obliged to depend on indoor activities when they tired of playing in the snow. We had been given a Mirror dinghy kit for Christmas by Mr Manning and his helpers from the paper mill. Philip and Terry wanted to build the Mirror dinghy and felt very important when I said that they would be responsible for building the boat. It was decided, with the agreement of the staff, to build it in the same room as I had built my Mirror. It was far too cold to build it in one of the buildings outside. This kit was a most valuable present as we were now starting our second year of sailing. It would enable the children to crew on a much easier boat to sail, especially in rougher conditions at sea, as it did not require so much weight to balance it as the Enterprise did.

In order to give those children who had learnt to swim at Eastbourne the previous summer the opportunity to improve their swimming standard and pass their test for sailing, we found that we could have the exclusive use of a small but ancient heated swimming pool at Folkestone. It would be available for one hour from five o'clock on Saturdays. It was only available because that was not a very popular time. Being rather ancient and due to be knocked down in the not too far distant future, the cost was very little. We readily accepted the offer. Although it came at an awkward time of day, it was a great success and enabled several more children to qualify.

Not all the children who passed their swimming test wanted to sail. One boy, Billy, came up to me one day and asked would I mind if he did not come sailing any more. I replied that I did not mind at all, it was entirely his choice. Out of curiosity, and wondering if I had put him off in some way, I asked him why he had made this decision. He replied that he thought we would all sail out to sea like speedboats, and then jump in the sea and have a good swim! I think he found the thought of racing in a light wind not very exciting. It was far safer for the children to sail in the club races as they could get used to sailing in windy conditions when there was a rescue boat on hand. One or two children were obviously frightened of the water and just did not like boats.

Meanwhile, Charlie was taking the opportunity given to him by the foul weather to complete his gold Duke of Edinburgh Award. He had to produce a diesel engine model aeroplane of at least 3ft wingspan that was able to take off from the ground. He also had to build a glider of 50in wingspan and fly it for a stated minimum duration. For the gold level, he had to have an independent judge and so I arranged that the local model aeroplane club would kindly supply a suitable person when he was ready to fly these planes. He had passed the other sections of the gold award. Richard, who was at Barkingside, had already completed the gold level and I had accompanied him when he was invited to Buckingham Palace to receive the award.

In February, the snow had melted but the rivers were running quite high. Running through the park there was the dried-up bed of a stream that we were told usually only flowed underground, but once in seven years it flowed on the surface. I had noticed that the drive crossed over the dried-up stream via an arched brick bridge, which had always seemed a bit unnecessary to me. One morning, after heavy rain, to my complete amazement, I saw a stream running fast under the bridge 2 or 3ft deep. We were all very fascinated with the sudden appearance of such a lively stream and I decided to make the most of it. I found two old prams in the shed and with the help of Charlie and Graham, we lashed two five-gallon oil drums to each pram for buoyancy. We made up some paddles and poles and let the older children who could swim have a paddle down the stream to see how far they got before capsizing. It was not very far and then they had to run back to the house for a warm bath and change of clothes. I don't think I was very popular with the laundry lady! It was great fun and even Milly, the cook, joined in. By the following Saturday the stream had subsided and all we could do was to float paper boats down the stream.

The building work for the new home in Canterbury was going ahead quite well and Eileen was making frequent visits to make sure that things were going according to the plans. The architect had promised that all the good features of Chilton Park would be embodied in the plans, and any new ideas would be included if practical. We would have separate buildings for Cedarwood and Pinewood groups, which would have room for 12 children each, as well as staff accommodation. The third block would provide individual bedrooms for eight teenage boys and girls as well as providing an office and accommodation for staff, and would have the games room and hobbies room attached to the building. On one occasion, Eileen discovered that the fanlight of the toilet windows on the ground floor opened at eye level onto the footpath, and would have been quite dangerous to people using the footpath, and this design fault was quickly corrected by the architects.

Owing to Bill's previous connections with the children's homes run by Kent County Council, we had been invited to take part in their annual competitions of football, cricket and table tennis. We had never met with much success in cricket or football events and I much admired the spirit of our teams who played with a smile on their faces despite some severe defeats. As we were a mixed home of all ages, we could not really 'select' a team, but it was a case of finding sufficient boys of the approximate age for the teams. However, in the case of table tennis, we did not have to select so large a team and by now our youngsters had the experience of playing in the league, as well as having had a lot of coaching from Bill and his friend Monty.

We played in the table tennis tournament finals at one of the larger children's homes in Kent where the superintendent was particularly keen on table tennis and the conditions were good. We were told that Anne was eligible to play in our team as she lived in a children's home, which was lucky for us as she was very good at table tennis and was to win the Kent under-13 title the next year. We were also fortunate to have Mark in the team, who showed such promise that he played for the Canterbury and District League in their under-15 table tennis team. Perhaps with all that talent it was not all that surprising that we won the cup. It was a truly team effort and they all 'played their hearts out' and in the end we won by a narrow margin. All the older children were thrilled with the result and it seemed to make up for all the heavy defeats at football and cricket. It was also a thankyou to Bill and Monty for all their coaching and belief they had in our team.

We had some rather sad news at the beginning of the year when we were told that one of our working girls, Wendy, was pregnant. She had been working in a home for the elderly, where she had been resident. The baby was due in May and Wendy wanted to keep the baby. When Eileen and I visited her in a mother and baby home, we found that she somewhat naturally assumed she could come back to Chilton Park with her baby. The social worker was worried about the influence Wendy would have on the younger children and the example her return would set for the other teenage girls. However, it was agreed that she could return, but she must be helped to take responsibility for the care of the baby and all that entailed. We placed her in Pinewood Group as Sheila was experienced in the care of young babies. The older children soon saw the restrictions and work that the baby made for Wendy. I feel it helped them to see that having a baby was not all glamour and joy for a young girl on her own. However, the baby was very much the centre of attention and love. Wendy stayed with us for a few months until a suitable placement could be found for her and the child. In retrospect, I think we did the right thing for Wendy. Fortunately, we did not have any other unwanted pregnancies in the home.

Charlie had by now completed all the sections of the gold standard Duke of Edinburgh Award and the Mayor of Canterbury came out to Chilton Park and presented the gold award to Charlie. While the Mayor was entertained with a cup of tea Charlie showed him the two planes he made for the gold award and explained the intricacies of flying them.

Both Charlie and I received invitations to attend at Buckingham Palace on July 11th when Charlie would be presented with his award. We both were very excited with this invitation and looked forward to the big day. I then had a surprise in the post one day, when I received a second letter inviting me to be one of 32 marshals at the reception on that day. The recipients would be divided into 32 regional groups and the marshals would each be responsible for a group. I accepted the invitation with some trepidation but felt very honoured.

The day for the presentations came and Charlie and I, in our best suits, took the train to London. On arrival at the Palace, we separated and I had to report at the Riding School. It was there that I was introduced to Lord Hunt who explained to me my task as a marshal. A boy and a girl from my group would be chosen by ballot to receive the awards from the Duke of Edinburgh on behalf of the group. My task, having been presented to the Duke of Edinburgh by Lord Hunt, was in turn to introduce the selected boy and girl to the Duke. Everything seemed to work as was planned. The Duke of Edinburgh chatted informally to a number of the boys and girls before moving on to the next group.

Charlie and I left the Palace among a vast crowd of very happy people who had all enjoyed a most memorable day and certainly a story to recount to their grandchildren. We had an uneventful journey home and then we were kept busy recounting our experiences to the staff and the children and also to Eileen and Anne. About two days later, I received a letter from Lord Hunt thanking me for my assistance as a marshal. I kept the letter as my memento of a very memorable day.

Earlier in the year, arrangements had been made for us to participate in an exchange visit for four French boys to spend a two-week holiday at Chilton Park later that summer. Four of our older girls were invited for a similar holiday in a childcare institution in the South of France. The visits were to take place during the summer holidays. To make space for the French boys, we sent the junior children off on their annual holiday to Ramsgate and were able to give the visitors a bedroom to themselves, on the first floor, immediately above the office.

When the time came, we drove to Lydd Airport, near Folkestone, where the four boys were handed over to us. The eldest was Claude, who was 15 years old. Henri and Louis were 12 years old and Anton, aged 11, was the youngest. All of the boys spoke some English and Claude was quite fluent, but Anton's English was the most difficult to understand, especially when he was in trouble, when he claimed he did not understand English. The boys soon settled in and we could see that they were going to be a handful!

The boys went out most days in small groups with our children to various coastal spots. On one occasion, Anton was in a group visiting the swimming pool and the children were duly told to wait for the staff member to have changed before they entered the pool. Not Anton! He changed quickly and jumped in the nearest end of the pool, which happened to be the deep end. As he could not swim, he was in immediate trouble. Fortunately, Joan was soon on the scene and pulled Anton to safety. We soon realised that we had to keep an eye on Anton at all times.

I took the four boys to St Lawrence cricket ground in Canterbury to watch a county cricket match as part of their education. When they did not understand what was happening they would ask me in a loud voice and the elderly gentlemen sitting nearby would turn round and glare at me. Of course, this would not happen nowadays as people are used to singing and shouting at cricket matches.

One day I told them that they would have their promised treat, the highlight of their holiday – a day in London. I said we would have to get up early in order to catch the train from Canterbury. The trip was a success and I did not lose anyone. The day after we had got back, I found the wall clock, normally mounted up high on the wall of the ballroom, was missing. On investigation the French boys admitted taking it and handed it back to me, saying, "When we go to Londres you say we have to get up early."

When the end of the visit came, I told the boys to pack up their belongings and tidy up the bedroom. I happened to be in the office later on and I heard bottles and other rubbish raining down on the concrete path outside the office window. It was the boys tidying their bedroom by chucking all their rubbish out of the window, so they then had the job of cleaning up the path under supervision. I had to be very firm with Anton as he was quite deviant and at the same time, we formed a relationship because I was creating boundaries for his behaviour, giving him security. When we said goodbye at the airport, Anton was crying his eyes out when I said goodbye to him. It was a shame I did not know him longer and I hope he was able to relate to an adult in the future to meet his needs. I had a soft spot for the lad despite his difficult behaviour.

Following the boys' departure back to France, our four girls were soon on their way to the South of France. Two sisters, Heather and Marina, together with Jenny and Leslie, had been chosen to go to France and they were all very excited for a week or two before the day of departure came. It was a great experience for them to go on holiday in such a small group and be amongst strangers. We saw the girls off from Lydd Airport and it was a completely new experience for them to go by aeroplane. The holiday went very well. The only complaint from the girls was that the French girls, insisted on trying on their visitors' clothes, even though they were one or two sizes larger!

Chapter 23

On Our Way

Work on the new home, on the site of an old orchard in Canterbury, had been started in November 1965, and was scheduled to be ready for our occupation in January 1967. During 1966, the staff and children had been aware of our new building being erected in Canterbury but we were more than occupied with our daily routine at Chilton Park. As the year progressed, our thoughts turned more and more to the new home, which would be ready for occupation after Christmas, subject to bad weather not causing a delay to the builders. The site was a particularly muddy one due to the clay soil.

The children wanted to know what we were going to call the new home. We asked them for suggestions and they came up with several names, the most popular one being 'Woodlands'. This was the most logical name as the three groups were named after trees. Now that the older children were in the group previously called Aspenwood, they wanted to change it to Oakwood, which we all agreed on. Headquarters had their own ideas about naming the new home, but to the children's delight they agreed on 'Woodlands'.

As we would be moving into Canterbury early in the New Year, it had been decided to move all the secondary school aged children who were not already going to schools in the city, into Canterbury schools at the beginning of the school year in September, 1966. The junior school children would, however, continue at the local school until we actually moved. The nearest junior school to us would be at Blean, on the outskirts of Canterbury, but within walking distance of the new home.

Eileen had, with some assistance, spent many hours measuring the windows for curtains. Then the house-mothers chose the materials for the curtains for their houses. It was decided that we would make as many of the curtains as possible and a local firm would make the rest. A lot of other decisions had to be made and fortunately, we had very good co-operation with the architects and the builders.

I had asked for a hard surfaced playing area the size of a tennis court that could be used for other games as well as tennis. There was an old wartime prefabricated bungalow in the grounds in a bad state of repair and it was decided that the builders would renovate it, leaving an empty shell that could be used as a store for our sailing boats. This would not only house our five dinghies, but would give us somewhere to work on the boats in the winter. The architects had designed a games room with a gallery where our model railway could be re-built. Underneath was a hobbies room and the remainder of the space would be used for table tennis and our small snooker table. I had a small battle on my hands regarding the floor surface as I asked for a wooden floor with a non-slippery surface, which would be safer for the children, but on economy grounds, a plastic floor covering would save a lot of money. A plastic floor tended to attract moisture, which, combined with the smooth surface of the plastic, could cause the children to slip. I was most grateful that I got my wooden floor in the end.

During the building period, we had constant visits from both the building department of Barnardo's and from the supplies department at Stepney. A lot of time was spent between Eileen and the staff with Mr Myer from Stepney. Decisions had to be made deciding which furniture would be taken with us and what would have to be replaced. Everything was geared towards a move soon after Christmas, and fortunately, as circumstances turned out, the builders were up to schedule.

At the beginning of November when I got out of bed one morning, the house felt unusually cold. I thought that the central heating boiler must have gone out during the night, but when I went down into the cellar, to my horror, I found the floor of the boiler room covered in some five or six inches of water. There appeared to have been an internal leak in the grate, which put out the fire and proceeded to leak out over the floor. A frantic call to headquarters' building department resulted in a prompt visit from Mr Wood. He confirmed that there was a leak in the boiler and said it would be too expensive to repair in view of our impending move to Canterbury.

Most of the ground floor rooms had a fireplace and we decided to light coke fires in these rooms to heat them. We had to use coke, which was in plentiful supply, now that one of the boilers was out of action. But first of all, we had to hunt out some fireguards for the children's rooms. Fortunately, we still had hot water, but I think we all felt a bit chilly! The kitchen with the Aga cooker was the warmest place in the house.

Hasty discussions were taking place between the builders and architects in Canterbury and with our architect's department and Miss Roots and her staff. It was decided that the best option would be to move into Canterbury as soon as was possible, and the builders would be asked to concentrate on the buildings to make them habitable and do the remainder of their work after we had moved in. Things moved very quickly and it was decided that we could actually move into Woodlands on Friday 2nd December. We could start moving furniture into the home from the beginning of that week.

November was a busy month and flashed by. We had the last fireworks display with the Round Table and then everyone was busy sorting out personal belongings and deciding what to take and what to discard. Curtain making had to be completed, and firms from whom furniture had been ordered were now given delivery dates. The removal firm had suggested that we would be allocated a van each day of the week. The first load would be non-essentials and gradually more essential items would be moved as the days went by, but culminating on the last night when the children would sleep on their mattresses on the floor. Their bedsteads would have been moved earlier on that day and would be assembled by the time the children arrived the next day.

Once the first load of furniture had arrived it was agreed that Eileen and I would sleep in Woodlands each night. We had our own accommodation in Oakwood, which consisted of a sitting room on the ground floor and upstairs we had three bedrooms and a bathroom, just separated by a door at the end of the corridor in which four girls' single bedrooms were situated. We were used to communal living but for Anne's sake we would have preferred a self-contained flat with a kitchen. The boys' three single rooms were on a mezzanine floor and at the end of the corridor there was an additional larger room for visiting older boys.

Monday morning came and was a typical cold November day and we had only just got the children off to school when the furniture van arrived. Eileen and I were up early as we had all the usual tasks to perform as well as supervising the move. It had been a very long day by the time we drove back to Woodlands for the night. The building site was all in darkness and seemed quite inhospitable when we unlocked the unfamiliar door to Oakwood. We went up to our bedroom and it was very cold, but fortunately, we had an electric fire. We decided to have a hot bath as the builders had switched on the hot water, but it was not to be – the bath plug that had been fitted to the end of the chain was the wrong size!

And so began a hectic week for all of us, which I will not forget in a hurry. We would not have managed so well had we not had a tremendous amount of help from the local Round Table. Their members came to Woodlands each evening and helped to move furniture into place and they changed all the plugs on the electrical equipment from the round pins to the 13-amp plugs.

On the Friday of our removal week, the final load of furniture, mainly mattresses and last items of food and other essential items kept back to the last load, went off to Woodlands. Meanwhile, the children had all gone off to school as usual and the older ones would go to Woodlands after school, while the juniors would be collected in the minibus and brought back to Woodlands. It was a very exciting day for them and they all managed to find their way back to Woodlands. I think we all had happy memories and felt a bit sad to say goodbye to Chilton Park.

Part Three:

Woodlands

Chapter 24

Christmas 1966 and a Royal Visit

After the move, we only had three weeks to prepare for Christmas and it would be a very different Christmas this year, partly due to different surroundings, and also there had been some changes of staff due to the move. A married couple, Kathleen and Tom, had been with us at Chilton Park with their two young boys for a short while in order to take over Cedarwood when we moved to Canterbury. Tom would pursue his normal work but would help Kathleen out at weekends, and Fay would be her assistant. Sheila had Joan assisting her in Pinewood and Oakwood had Pam and Edna as their staff. We also had three 16-year-old girls, Noreen, Jenny and Celia, who were non-resident and came in daily. They assisted in the houses and were a great help. They also had the opportunity of learning more about childcare while they were too young for the post of assistant house-mother. Bill had moved back to work for Kent County Council, as he preferred to work in a larger home where he was more involved in sporting activities. Mary and Jean had also left us.

Whilst we had been very busy with burst boilers and moving house, Barnardo's had acquired a large bungalow nearby which would be used as a foster home for four working boys and girls. This unit would be run by a married couple, Mr and Mrs Browne.

Mr Browne would be at work and the foster unit would operate in conjunction with Woodlands.

Eileen had a lot of re-organising the ordering of food and supplies now we had three separate units. I could see I would be kept busy in the garden as we were not employing a gardener and there were two acres of grounds to maintain. I had told headquarters that if they had the land grassed over I could maintain it and then develop the grounds as I required. Christmas was upon us before we were ready but we were glad to have some central heating again. Naturally, in a new building, there were bound to be snags, especially as we had rather rushed the builders to let us in early. The first problem came up on Christmas Eve when we returned from the midnight service with some of the staff and one or two of our old boys and girls who had come for the holiday. As we got near to Woodlands, we were concerned to hear the fire alarm going off at full blast. Happily, it was a false alarm. However, we could not stop it ringing without turning it off completely. Unfortunately, the alarm had kept all the children awake, just when Father Christmas was due to make his rounds. Tired as we were, there was nothing for it but to delay Father Christmas with cups of coffee until the children were asleep.

With Christmas and the New Year's Eve party over, we were all busy adapting to a change of living accommodation and routines. The builders came back to the site after their traditional one week Christmas and New Year break, to a list of items that wouldn't work or needed adjustment. These were the sort of problems that anyone moving into a new house would find, except that in this case the building was more extensive and we had rushed the builders to let us move in at rather short notice. They had really done very well and their work had been up to schedule.

When it was proposed to build the home on the site at the end of a quiet cul-de-sac, there had been the usual complaints from residents at the thought of having lots of rough noisy children running around, and also of losing their view of the cathedral. Once the builders had started, there were numerous complaints from the local people that their drive entrances were blocked by the builders' cars. I decided to have an open weekend as soon as possible for the local residents so they would see that we had the facilities to occupy the children, and the staff to look after them properly. They would see the interiors were nicely furnished to make a homely feel about the place. I assured them that if they had any complaints, to come and see me and we would endeavour to look into the problem. We were not really ready to be showing people around but it was more important to build up good relationships locally and in time I am sure it paid off.

Eileen, Anne and I were now settling into our new home, Oakwood, along with three boys, four girls and two members of staff. The girls were Marina and Heather, who were sisters, and Leslie and Jenny. The boys were Graham and two brothers, Phillip and Terry. They were absolutely thrilled with their single bedrooms and the girls especially enjoyed adding individual touches. It gave the adolescents a feeling of privacy and independence. We had two house-mothers who worked in Oakwood, Elaine and Pamela, who enjoyed working with adolescents.

Canterbury and District Table Tennis League had their tournament in the New Year and Jenny and Anne did particularly well, winning several cups between them. After all the excitement of the move and of Christmas, life settled down to a new routine, but not for long.

In February, Cathleen had her 21st birthday party at Oakwood, which was enjoyed by all the older children. Cathleen had wanted to be a hairdresser when she left Chilton Park but had later trained as a nurse. On Christmas morning, I had driven over to Ashford, a nearby town, to collect Cathleen after she had been on night duty, and we had arranged the party during her visit.

Later in February, I had a telephone call from the general secretary with the exciting news that Princess Margaret, President of Barnardo's, would visit Woodlands. The Princess had agreed to officially open the home on 3rd May. This news had many implications, not the least was the liasing with headquarters' staff and local officials. Eileen and I had recently booked a week's holiday in a chalet on the Norfolk Broads. Our first instinct was to cancel the holiday, but we really felt we needed a break after the upheaval of the past few months and we knew we would be back more than a month before the visit. In fact the visit was very much on our minds and prevented us from enjoying the holiday as much as we had hoped. Although it rained quite a lot, we were able to rest, but each night I had vivid dreams of all that could go wrong during the visit. We returned to Canterbury refreshed and ready for action.

One morning, I had a telephone call from the squadron leader in charge of the Queen's Flight. He asked for a map reference for a landing site near to Woodlands. He said that he would be doing a proving flight in two days' time. Very close to Woodlands were two boys' public schools and it seemed to me that their playing fields would make excellent landing grounds. I approached the nearest one about half a mile away and spoke to the bursar. He said that his headmaster was away at the headmasters' conference and he could not give agreement for the royal helicopter to land, without referring it to his headmaster.

Another half mile away was the other school and in answer to my request to the bursar, he also said that his headmaster was away at the conference. To my delight, he was prepared to take the responsibility and agreed to the helicopter landing on the playing fields. I told him the time the helicopter would land and that I had been told to pin a white marker of some sheets to mark the exact spot. Back at Woodlands, I was grateful for the practice at map reading and map references which I had experienced helping the children with their Duke of Edinburgh Awards. I also had to give the squadron leader information on any hazards near the landing ground such as overhead wires.

The builders were told of the forthcoming royal visit and its implications for them. It was quite good to spur them to finish the job and tidy up the site. It was requested that a room and a bathroom should be made available for Princess Margaret's personal use. It was decided to use rooms in our flat upstairs in Oakwood. The builder immediately decided to put on a better quality lock on our bathroom door! We went out and bought a small stool for the dressing table covered in red-coloured velvet, which we thought was suitable for royalty.

Besides the VIPs and local dignitaries, Barnardo's invited

numerous people in Kent who gave their time to support the organisation with fund raising. A marquee was to be erected in the grounds where we had a grass area for playing croquet. People who received an invitation to attend would have tea served in the marquee whilst Princess Margaret was touring the buildings and having tea. When Her Highness departed, they were invited to look round the home. The VIPs, including the Mayor, would have tea in Oakwood. The staff thought it would be a nice idea if the Princess could have tea with the children as it was a private visit to the home. A request for this was made to Kensington Palace and to everyone's delight, it was granted. A local school of catering gladly accepted the invitation to serve the refreshments to the VIPs in Oakwood and to the children and staff who had tea in the games room with the Princess. We were informed that we would have to write to Kensington Palace and request a permit to obtain the special blend of tea used by the royal family. We also were told to prepare brown bread sandwiches of smoked salmon for the Princess.

Of course, Eileen had to have a new outfit for the occasion, which naturally she did not object to! However, there was a snag, as Eileen did not like wearing a hat and in fact did not even possess one. She was expected to wear a hat for the occasion so she went out and bought the minimum – a small hat composed mainly of feathers. It all looked very nice in the end and Eileen felt more comfortable. In the weeks before the royal visit, the children were full of excitement and anticipation about the event. A lot of discussion centred around what they should wear and a few purchases were made as the clothing allowance permitted. The children tidied their rooms and the staff made extra sure that everything was cleaned and polished. The children were also enjoying a lot of attention from their school friends who wanted to know details of the coming event.

The great day, May 3rd, arrived, and as far as we could tell, everything was in place. The builders had done very well to tidy up Woodlands and make it look presentable. The staff at headquarters had done an excellent job making all the necessary arrangements and had made an exact schedule of precise timings and places where each individual would meet the Princess. Of course, they had done this sort of thing many times before for our president's visits. On this occasion, the Princess was visiting a Barnardo's nursery nurse training school in Tunbridge Wells in the morning, and coming by helicopter to Canterbury in the afternoon.

Princess Margaret was due to arrive at 3.40pm. By 3.30, everyone was ready, although we still awaited the arrival of the Mayoress. The red carpet was placed in position on the forecourt and also where the Princess would walk when being introduced to a welcoming group of people. Although it was a fine day, there was quite a gusty wind, which kept curling up the carpet. After a hasty discussion, it was decided, for safety reasons, to do away with the carpet on the forecourt. Some 400 guests had been invited and they filled the forecourt and others watched through the windows of the buildings facing onto this area. Local people in the cul-de-sac had requested invitations but I had to refuse them as all the places we were allowed had been allocated. It would in some way have compensated them for all the problems that they had experienced with builders' cars, but I think that they were able to see quite a lot from their gardens. As the time for the arrival of the helicopter drew near, anxious eyes were scanning the skyline for a sight of the royal plane. Just before it was sighted, to everyone's relief, the Mayoress arrived to join the Mayor at the gate and the official party was ready to welcome the Princess.

Meanwhile, at the school, the boys and staff had lined the playing field to see the arrival of the Princess. The helicopter landed just seven minutes late, and the Princess was greeted by Barnardo's officials and the headmaster and his wife. The party then travelled in a fleet of cars the short distance to Woodlands through roads crowded with people trying to catch a glimpse of the Princess.

As Princess Margaret got out of the car at the entrance gates, the first thing she did was to quietly ask the accompanying plain-clothes policeman to find out who had won the 2000 Guineas race! Her Royal Highness was wearing an elegant knee-length green outfit with what was referred to as a 'jelly bag' hat, which was gathered at the sides into large gold-coloured hoops. This hat caused a lot of comments during the afternoon. The Princess was then welcomed by the Mayor and Mayoress and the town clerk and his wife, before proceeding across the forecourt – now without its red carpet – to where the Princess was introduced to some Barnardo's officials and to Eileen and myself – a very proud moment for both of us. Before the Princess arrived, we had stood on the red carpet which was placed in front of us for the Princess to walk on, in order to stop it from rumpling up and being displaced. However, we all failed to get off it at the moment of the introductions and consequently we stood on the red carpet and the Princess walked on the paving stones! I wonder what she thought!

After the introductions were completed, Eileen and I led the Princess, with her lady-in-waiting, and both the chairman and general secretary of the Barnardo's council on a tour of the buildings. It had been decided that owing to the narrow corridors, the rest of the party, including the Mayor and Mayoress and the town clerk and his wife, would follow at a 'discreet distance'. It was the first official visit of Princess Margaret to Canterbury and there was some feeling that the Mayor was relegated to the second half of the touring party and also that he was not invited to tea with Her Royal Highness. However, it was pointed out that this was a private visit and he was invited out of courtesy.

We first of all visited Cedarwood and the Princess met the house-parents in their flat, before going upstairs to the bedrooms. In one bedroom, Princess Margaret chatted to three girls who were playing Monopoly. In another bedroom she chatted to three younger boys. The boys were with a student from a residential childcare course, who was with us for a month on her practical placement. She would have a tale to tell the other students when they got together for their next term at college! Downstairs in the lounge, the Princess met a house-mother and four children, and in the dining room, she was introduced to representatives of the builders, surveyors and the architects, including Barnardo's chief architect. The three assistant house-mothers were waiting to greet the Princess as she went out through the kitchen. The Princess discussed their work with them and asked if they were happy in their work at Woodlands. Fortunately, they said yes!

The party proceeded to Pinewood, where the Princess was greeted by the house-mother in charge. In the dining room, she met representatives of the local Barnardo's Helpers League, who worked so hard to raise money for the society. In the lounge were four young children with a house-mother, while upstairs there were five boys with another house-mother. In the next room, Princess Margaret spoke to Wendy, the single mother, who had moved with us from Chilton Park. Wendy proudly showed her son to the Princess remarking that he was exactly one year old to the day.

Coming out of Pinewood, we pointed out the tennis court that could be used both for tennis and other games, especially in winter. We also drew the Princess' attention to the large shed used to store our boats and where there was room to work on the boats during the winter. We passed a Mirror dinghy, which had been built by two boys, Phillip and Graham, from a kit given to us by Mr Manning and his helpers at the paper mill. The Princess showed a keen interest in the boat and had a chat with the boys who built it, remarking as she moved on, "I hope it works." It was going to do just that indeed, for Phillip, with Marina as crew, was going to sail this boat in the Mirror national championships at Plymouth later on in the year.

We continued over to Oakwood and showed the Princess the three single bedrooms for the older boys and a larger bedroom for working boys coming back to visit, often to visit their younger brothers and sisters. Upstairs, she was shown the four single bedrooms for the girls, and at the end of the corridor, our flat, consisting of three bedrooms and a bathroom. We told the Princess how much the older children valued their single rooms. In the dining room, the Princess met the house-mother with the four older girls and my daughter, Anne, and in the dining area were more Barnardo's officials. The last group waiting to meet the Princess was in our sitting room and consisted of the foster parents who ran the Barnardo's foster home nearby, and the four teenagers for whom they were responsible. These young people had moved from Woodlands when they started work and this foster home provided them with the support they needed at this time. One girl was a mother's help, one was a trainee nurse and the third girl worked in the cashier's office of a large insurance firm. The fourth youngster was an apprentice chef at a local restaurant.

Time was going by very quickly and the visit was scheduled only to take an hour and a half. We now showed the Princess into the games room where all the children and staff were seated at small tables, waiting patiently for her arrival and eagerly looking at the food. Princess Margaret sat at a table with her lady-in-waiting, two Barnardo's officials and Eileen and myself. When the plate of brown bread smoked salmon sandwiches were passed to the Princess, she took one and had a quick peep inside, to make sure, presumably, that it was smoked salmon. We had been asked to have an empty chair beside the Princess so either staff or children could come up while she ate her tea and chat to her. It was easy to get staff to volunteer but the children were rather shy. In the end, one of our old girls who was getting married to a fireman the following week agreed to come, and we got Anne to volunteer to make up the numbers.

As the time drew near for Princess Margaret to depart, children and staff assembled on the forecourt to wave goodbye to the Princess along with some of the visitors who managed to crowd round the edge. Princess Margaret had been asked to plant a catalpa tree by the front door to commemorate her visit. She had happily agreed to this and it was now time for the planting to take place. She was handed a shiny spade that was kindly lent to us by the police for this occasion. This spade was a gardening trophy awarded to the local police. Jill, being the youngest girl in Woodlands, then presented a posy to the Princess, which she accepted graciously before departing in her car on the way back to the helicopter.

After Princess Margaret had departed, we then socialised with the many remaining guests and after a while said farewell to the Mayor and Mayoress and their party, and the official representatives from Barnardo's. Gradually, the crowds thinned down and Woodlands returned to some semblance of normality. We then had the opportunity to speak with the children and staff and find out what they thought of the visit. As we had hoped, they were all thrilled with the events of the day and the children were anxious to recount the treasured moments when they'd actually had a conversation with the Princess. Soon it was time for the younger children to settle in their own houses and quieten down before bedtime.

We were just beginning to relax when a reporter from the BBC radio arrived to record our reactions to the visit, especially those of the children. I must say that my heart was in my mouth wondering what the children might say. However, it all went very well and I recall one 12-year-old boy being asked what he thought of the Princess. He replied, "What big earrings she had." He had thought the large hoops on the hat Princess Margaret was wearing were her earrings!

Late that night we sat down with some of the staff and reviewed the day and we agreed we could quietly congratulate ourselves that all had gone very well and we had avoided any major slip-ups. The children had behaved impeccably and the staff had been superb in their support.

In due course, we received a letter from Princess Margaret's lady-in-waiting saying how much the Princess had enjoyed the visit and that she was "particularly pleased to hear about the careful steps taken to bridge the difficult gap between childhood in the home and an independent adult life outside it."

This memorable and happy event is frequently recalled when we see many of these children who are now mature adults.

Eileen watches as Barney is introduced to Princess Margaret
Photo reproduced with permission of the Kentish Gazette

Princess Margaret speaks to the boys who built the boat
Photo by Kentish Observer who ceased publication in the 1970s. Now untraceable.

Games room with table tennis and snooker table

After Barnardo's Regatta with trophies

Mirror dinghy no. 7611 built by the children and sailed at Plymouth

Christmas entertainment

Christmas fun

Chapter 25

Sailing and Weddings

Life continued to be hectic after the royal visit. Maria, who had sat and chatted to Princess Margaret at teatime during her visit, was married to a fireman a month later. The wedding took place at our local church, where her three sisters were bridesmaids and the reception was held in Oakwood, much to everyone's delight.

Eileen had been made a governor of Archbishop's Secondary Modern School and that year I was invited to present the prizes at sports day. Chatting to the teachers afterwards, one remarked how much Phillip's maths had improved, since the boys had learned to sail. He said that when he started to talk about navigation during the maths lesson, Phillip had shown much more interest in the subject. Graham's English teacher remarked that Graham had written a very good essay about an imaginary voyage across the ocean in a boat. It showed how the sailing had given the youngsters both an interest and self-confidence.

Eileen and I had discussed with the Oakwood group the subject of holidays and a popular idea was to enter the Mirror dinghy in the national championships at Plymouth in August. We would also take my boat and trail the two boats, one upside down, on top of the other. We had by now acquired a Ford Zephyr saloon car and we could manage to seat four in the back seat and three in the front. We had a very large boot which could hold all of our personal luggage and our sailing gear would have to go in the dinghy. Marina and her sister Heather, and Phillip and his brother Terry, were all very keen to come. Anne also wanted to come and crew with me and so there would just be room for all of us. We had to nominate the same crew, each day, for the week of the national championships, but if we went down to Plymouth for two weeks, we could sail in the Plymouth regatta week as well. The regatta was held the week before the nationals and in these races the crew could change daily if necessary. It was agreed that Philip would be the skipper of the dinghy he had helped to build, for both weeks. During the regatta week, Heather and Terry would take turns to crew, and Marina would crew during the nationals week. Anne said she wanted to crew both weeks but if necessary one of the others could take her place in the first week.

The next step was to find economical accommodation and we finally settled on a small holiday camp a few miles outside Plymouth where we could have the use of three chalets. The camp had a swimming pool and this made it a very popular choice.

It would be a long journey to Plymouth and so we decided to start on the Friday about midday and so take advantage of driving through the night. We had to limit our speed because of the boats we were trailing, but the journey went smoothly and we were able to make some stops for refreshments and to stretch our legs. Twice I stopped for a longer break so that I could have a refreshing nap. I had been given clear instructions and I was able to find the camp without much difficulty early on Saturday morning, after an uneventful drive. There was one problem, as Phillip pointed out – the car had a list to port. It appeared that the rear near-side spring had broken. I visited a nearby garage who were Ford dealers, while the rest of the party sorted out our belongings. The garage confirmed that we needed a new pair of springs due to overloading the car. They suggested that they replaced the springs with 'police springs'. Apparently, these were fitted to police Ford cars carrying heavy radar speed trap equipment. They promised to have the car ready for me before the end of the day. It was fortunate that we had arrived early on Saturday and we would be able to take the boats down to the harbour that evening after we had had some rest.

The regatta races were hosted in turn by various sailing clubs round the Sound, including the air sea rescue unit on Mountbaten Breakwater. It appeared that a number of Mirror sailors had decided to use the regatta races to get used to the local conditions and so we had a turn out of about 20 boats and our own start. Weather conditions were very good for the first few days, giving us time to get used to sailing in different conditions to those we were used to in Kent. By the end of the week, the wind had picked up and was accompanied by rain. By now, Philip had gained confidence sailing in different surroundings and both of our boats were going well. We did not manage to win any prizes in the regatta except for a third place I won on one occasion. Philip had finished consistently in the middle of the fleet. By the end of the regatta week we all felt ready to participate in the biggest races in which we had ever taken part, both in importance and numbers. There were over 120 entries, with more than 100 mirror dinghies taking part each day in the national championships.

The first race of the nationals was designated as a practice race – some practice! It nearly resulted in the end of the racing for Philip and his crew. We woke up on that Sunday morning to a strong wind and arrived at the dinghy park to see white horses in Plymouth Sound. As it was a practice race and in view of the weather – force four to five forecast – the organisers said the race would be held on an inshore course. Philip was eager to sail in these conditions and so was Anne. We both got to the start all right but then the wind picked up and we were later informed it was gusting force six. Anne and I soon found that we filled up with water coming over the sides on our beating to windward, and as soon as we came off the wind, we had to bail vigorously in order to get the boat moving. The Mirror dinghy was a very safe boat, with four built-in buoyancy compartments. It was virtually unsinkable but did not sail very well when full of water. Besides a bailer, I had a plastic bucket on board so we could both bail and get the boat moving again.

Each time we came round the course near to shore, I asked Anne if she wanted to go ashore but she wanted to stick it out and finish the race. She was a very good swimmer and did not show any fear of the water. We both went ashore with a feeling of satisfaction at having completed the race, but we did not come near to the front. Anne was a great benefit in calm conditions due to her light weight but in windy situations she was a little on the light side.

I had hardly come ashore, when a worried looking Philip came up to me and said he had broken the mast of the Mirror dinghy. As 13 boats had broken their masts and the mobile spares shop in the dinghy park had only 12 masts, he had booked one and said his uncle would pay for it when he came ashore. I instantly allayed his fears and said he had done the right thing and I praised his initiative. We would be able to claim the cost of the mast from the insurers. Apparently, the masts had failed due to a compression fracture and had not actually broken but had lost their rigidity.

After the traumas of the practice race, things were slightly more calm, both the boats finishing about the middle of the fleet. On one occasion, while jostling for position on the start line, rather too near one of the two buoys denoting the starting line, I hit a buoy trying to avoid another boat, which squeezed me onto it. For such an offence I was immediately disqualified from that race and had to return to the dinghy park, much to my crew's disgust. We had one good result when we finished in the top ten.

After two weeks of holidays and sailing, we were ready to return home, which we did without incident, and our 'police springs' worked very well. For Marina and Heather it was farewell to sailing as they were to return home with their two younger brothers, in two weeks' time.

Christmas 1967 was celebrated in each house separately, but in Oakwood we invited the older ones from Cedarwood and Pinewood to join in the New Year fancy dress party. Four of our visitors, old boys Philip, Tom and Charlie and old girl Sally, entertained us by forming an impromptu band. Philip played the drums, Charlie and Tom played guitars, and Sally supplied the vocal talent. Three of the house-mothers added a colourful spectacle as the three wise men. Eighteen of our youngsters and a number of staff joined in the fun. Eileen wore a blonde wig of shoulder length hair, dark glasses and a skimpy pink dress. The boys did not recognise Eileen and called her the 'pink bit of stuff' and were quite impressed with their visitor!

By the spring of 1968, there had been a turn around of the young-sters living in Oakwood, and by now all the girls had left to return to their families, except for Jenny. Their places were taken up by three new girls, Gill, Penny and Wendy, who came direct to Oakwood. Philip had left school, and wanted to be an agriculture engineer. His place was taken up by Sam who came to us direct from another Barnardo's home.

Sam was an intelligent boy who had extreme difficulties at school, lazy, but with a lovely sense of humour. I gave him the opportunity to build the second Mirror dinghy kit that we had been given. I told him that he was in charge and it was up to him to recruit help from the other boys. At first, his assistants did not last very long and it was an exercise in relationships for him, but he soon learnt to work as a team, as well as being team leader. There was one hiccup, when he came to me, looking a bit sheepish, and said he had a problem. He showed me two port sides he had made up, instead of one port and one starboard side. He looked rather surprised when I didn't tell him off but told him that he would have to come with me and find a timber yard selling waterproof plywood. It was quite useful to have some spare plywood for mending damage to the boats in the future. Sam managed to finish the boat and we called it 'Mirocal' because he managed to complete it and it did not sink! Later on, when the woodwork teacher at Sam's school started to build a Mirror dinghy from a kit, Sam was able to advise his teacher what to do. With this new found confidence, Sam seemed to enjoy the remainder of his school days.

Sam took a particular interest in gardening at school and was soon asking me to spare him some room in my greenhouse so that he could grow some plants. I was delighted in his new interest and enthusiasm and was happy to comply, although I had filled the greenhouse with melon plants and had been able to supply melons for all three houses. When we went on holiday that year, I had to ask Auntie Pam from Oakwood to pollinate the melon plants, much to everyone's amusement. I had planted up a fruit garden of raspberries and strawberries for the benefit of us all. Meanwhile, some of the children were asking if they could have individual gardens and we had plenty of room for these once we had made a decision of where to put them.

I now found myself quite busy maintaining the grounds. I usually did this in the afternoon when I found it was a relaxing break. We had a footpath running from the main road to the back of our houses, which was used as a short cut by the residents of Woodlands. In the winter-time it was rather dark and badly lit and Barnardo's agreed that we could have a light on the corner of the boat shed. I came to an agreement with the contractor that if I dug the trench for the cable to run from the rear of Oakwood he would put in a heavy duty cable at no extra cost so that we could run power tools in the boat shed. I don't know who got the best bargain but at the time it felt that the contractor had! The trench was about 120yds long and it was a very heavy clay soil. I used to do an hour or two each afternoon and by the time I finished digging, I had tennis elbow quite badly in my right arm. One afternoon I was digging away when a social worker passed by with a teenage girl who was being considered for admission to Oakwood. We were introduced by the social worker and I followed them indoors in order to have a wash and change my clothes. When I appeared in the office where the social worker and her charge were talking to Edna the house-mother and Eileen, Edna helpfully said to the girl, "This is Mr Butler, the superintendent." The confused girl replied, "I have met Mr Butler, the gardener, but not Mr Butler, the superintendent."

We entered two Mirror dinghies, including mine, in a weekend regatta at Deal. After the first race on each day, we would eat our sandwiches for lunch and then we would have the second race of the day. The weather was just right for sailing until after lunch on Sunday, when Philip asked if he could launch their Mirror for the final race. I noted that one or two boats were being launched and the rescue boat was getting ready. I told Philip and Terry that they could go ahead and a few minutes after they launched, a vicious squall blew up and whisked them straight out to sea. Fortunately, Philip did not panic and did not attempt to turn back until the wind had lessened. As it was, sailing was cancelled and the results were declared for just the three races completed. To my surprise, I had come third and won a handy saw for cutting a variety of materials. The boys were most amused and thought I had been given it as a hint that my boat was useless and I should cut up my boat.

Anne had by now caught the sailing bug and was ready to helm her own boat in club races, and I wanted a larger boat that gave me more of a challenge. I decided to buy a Mirror 16, which, as its name implies, was a development of the Mirror dinghy, and was 16ft long. It had a folding canvas dodger, a secure place to fit an outboard motor under the fore deck and a single burner stove and storage for supplies under the side decks. It had a double floor, the inside one being flat, and up to four people could sleep comfortably on the floor. Also, this made the boat self-draining, in the event of the boat capsizing. When the cruising equipment was removed, the boat could be raced with a performance equivalent to that of a Wayfarer dinghy. I decided to order a Mirror 16 from the builders who were in Leicester, and was told delivery would be in July.

We had discussed at recent staff meetings the subject of the children's summer holidays and had decided that we would organise a seaside holiday for Cedarwood and Pinewood at Ramsgate, using a church hall for accommodation. The Oakwood youngsters were keen to take up our suggestion that they should go on holiday in pairs. They would have a choice of Outward Bound type holidays, which would give them the experience of travelling on their own and mixing with other youngsters. Eileen would organise the holiday at Ramsgate and take Anne with her for the two weeks. I would be left at Woodlands with just some of the Oakwood youngsters who were not on holiday and the two house-mothers, Edna and Pam. The weekend in the middle of the fortnight was one I had planned to take some of the boys on a sailing weekend with the sailing club.

The sailing club at Tankerton had an annual weekend away in August when club members sailed in company to the Isle of Sheppey, and slept in tents on the beach at Queenborough. The members would sail back to Tankerton the next day. I had decided to take the Enterprise with Graham as crew and Philip, who was not working at the weekend, would sail in a Mirror with his brother Terry. I would take tents and supplies for all of us in the Enterprise. A single letter through the letterbox at the beginning of the week changed all my plans. It was a letter from the boatyard informing me that my Mirror 16 was ready for collection. I suppose some people would describe me as an optimist to the extreme, but it was a most memorable weekend as it turned out.

I decided that the Mirror 16 was more suitable for the cruise and I could go up to Leicester to collect it on the Friday, the day before the cruise. When I suggested the idea to the boys, they were all very keen and wanted to come with me to Leicester. On the Friday morning, Graham, Terry and Sam set off with me about 7am. Complete with sandwiches and a promise to Edna and Pam that we would be back by six or seven o'clock that evening for our tea. It was, after all, a journey that I was quite familiar with, travelling up to London, over Vauxhall Bridge, and across to South Mimms where we would soon join the M1 motorway to Leicester. It was a journey of about 150 miles each way and I expected to return through London before the evening rush hour commenced.

The boys thoroughly enjoyed the journey in the Ford Zephyr car and we made good time. The boat was all ready for me when I arrived at the boat builder's yard, with one exception. They had forgotten to supply the fittings to secure the outboard motor. We had to hang about the yard while they glued and screwed on the fittings. And then they had to varnish the new parts. Meanwhile, we took the opportunity to eat our packed lunches. Unfortunately, the delay meant that we were driving through London about seven o'clock, just after the rush hour, but we were in the theatre traffic. The problem was getting into the correct traffic lane whilst towing a 16ft-long boat, without side swiping the car behind me with my trailer. The journey home also took longer because of towing a trailer. We arrived home much to the house-mothers' relief, about half-past nine. We were all tired, but the boys had enjoyed the drive and the visit to the boat yard. They were also excited at seeing the new boat, especially Graham who would be crewing it the next day if all went well. I think we all slept well that night.

Saturday morning came and we got up to a not very inviting day.

It was dull and cloudy and not very warm for August. We set off to Tankerton after a cooked breakfast, wondering what was in store for us. Graham and Terry came with me and we met Philip at the club. He was already preparing the Mirror, and other club members were also preparing their boats. There was considerable interest in my new boat but I was trying to read the instructions for rigging it in the rain and the paper was getting wet. I was not used to roller reefing for the foresail and this took some sorting out. I did not bother to rig the spinnaker as we were only cruising and not racing. I fitted the brand new outboard motor into its place in the bow. By now the fleet of club boats had departed and I said I would catch them up. At last, I considered we had rigged the boat properly and checked that we knew which ropes to pull and so were ready to set sail. It was still raining and the wind was light, the latter being helpful as we were sailing an unknown boat and did not want any surprises. On the other hand, the club boats had departed at a time that would enable them to catch the tide where the Medway flowed into the Thames, just before they would reach Queenborough. We would be too late to catch the tide and would be sailing against it unless the wind picked up.

The wind remained light and so we struggled against the tide as we neared our destination. I got out our new outboard motor, which I had topped up with fuel before we started, and pulled the starting cord a few times, and just before I was about to give up, it burst into life. I was so relieved, as time was getting along and we were not making any progress against the tide. As we turned a corner, we caught up with a Mirror dinghy from the club struggling to make any progress. We threw them a rope and took the dinghy in tow and our trusty outboard still made progress. We soon came across the other boats and tents on the side of the river and joined them. We moored up alongside a barge and had a comfortable night. Next day, on Sunday, we sailed back on the inshore side of the island, and had to wait for the road and rail bridge to open to let us through. We had to hoist a bucket up the mast to signify that we wanted to get past the bridge. After short while, the traffic stopped either side of the bridge and it slowly opened up. We all felt quite important that the traffic had to stop to let us pass.

We eventually returned home after our adventures over the past three days. We had been fortunate that everything had gone well, including the weather, and importantly, the boys had something to remember that was different to normal everyday life. I expected some good essays would be written at school based on our adventures.

I had entered the Mirror 16 in the national championships, organised by Thorpe Bay Sailing Club, near to Southend-on Sea. There would be four races, sailed over a weekend, and we could bring a tent and pitch it on the club grounds. Eileen was coming to look after our domestic needs and support us, and Graham was thrilled to be sailing the new boat. We arrived on Friday evening and pitched our tent and unpacked before joining some of our fellow participants in the club house. The club was situated on an open shingle beach rather like the conditions we were used to at Tankerton and so we felt at home.

The first race sailed on Saturday morning was sailed in light winds, force two to three on the Beaufort scale. We were not too sure of ourselves for the first race, did not hear the 'ten minute gun' and had a bad start. There were 16 boats in the race and we finished in ninth place. In the afternoon, after a good lunch in the clubhouse, we had our second race, sailed in similar conditions to the morning race. This time we made sure we concentrated more, and we managed a better start and finished in fourth place. We spent a sociable evening in the clubhouse and I got to know the representative of the Daily Mirror who was responsible for all the publicity connected with their sponsorship of the Mirror dinghies.

Sunday morning was cloudy, somewhat cooler, and both rain and increasing wind were forecast. We had a good start in the first race and were soon in second position following a boat that was sailed by two brothers who had built it themselves and only finished it a week before the nationals. Graham was doing very well and we held on to achieve second place. One boat capsized and it was apparent that the wind was getting stronger. The two brothers won the race and this put them firmly in the leading position with one race to go. As we could all discard our worst result, in our case a ninth position, things were looking quite good for us if we could discard that result and get a good place in the last race. After another enjoyable lunch, we prepared for the final race. The wind was now reaching a good force four and gusting more, and as a result of one boat capsizing in the previous race, everyone was reefing their sails. The Mirror 16 had a large sail area that could be reefed and also it had a low aspect sail plan, that is the mast was slightly shorter than most dinghies of that size. I discussed the situation with Graham and said that we could have a good result if we did not reef the sails, but we took the chance of capsizing, and a bad result. Capsizing was not a great issue as we practised righting a boat after having capsized, and in any case, there was a rescue boat in attendance. We decided to 'go for it'. With a fairly careful start, we got down to business and found we could just manage our full rig, and we soon found ourselves in the lead. Towards the end of the race, we were both feeling the strain, our muscles aching and a danger of losing concentration, a frequent cause of capsizing. I kept shouting encouragement to Graham and he managed to complete the race; we had come first and the two brothers were second. The two brothers won the event and we had come second overall. I won a trophy for winning that race and a pair of binoculars for second place overall. It was a great achievement for both of us and Graham had played a most important part. Well done Graham!

It had been a most exciting weekend for us and we had done much better than we had ever dreamed. Our excitement was brought down to earth on the journey home when a wheel bearing on the boat trailer seized up. I had to leave the boat on the forecourt of a nearby garage while we drove back to Canterbury, hitched up my other trailer, which we used for smaller boats, and returned to the Mirror 16. The trailer had broken down not far outside Southend and so it was quite late when I eventually arrived home with the boat.

In September, we were busy preparing for another wedding. Milly, one of a family of five, had been with us at Chilton Park. Her younger sister, Dawn, was still with us and was to be bridesmaid. Although Milly had left us a few years before, she was still in touch and asked for the reception to be at Woodlands, and we were delighted to agree. This was another happy occasion enjoyed by the staff and the children.

Chapter 26

1968 – Another Change in Sight

When we were attending a meeting for heads of homes at our area office at Tunbridge Wells, Eileen and I had another shock. We were told that Barnardo's had done some research of future childcare needs and this had shown that the trend would be towards specialist homes and concentration of resources in urban areas, where the need would be the greatest. We were told that due to a new regionalisation policy, Barnardo's would be withdrawing from the Canterbury area unless we could suggest a change of use for Woodlands that would justify keeping the home open. We were stunned and drove back home in a daze. After the shock of being told suddenly that Chilton Park was closing down, we had spent two years planning Woodlands. Now, two-and-a-half years after moving, just as we had felt settled in, we were expected to think of another use for the home. The home had been specifically designed for its present purpose. We would not unsettle the staff or children until a definite decision was made. Meanwhile, we must consider an alternative use for Woodlands while carrying on our work as usual, and not letting these plans distract us from our work.

Miss Roots had asked me when I was going to apply for the advanced course in residential childcare and suggested that I should apply to Barnardo's for secondment. The course was held at both Newcastle and Bristol Universities and lasted a year. I was loath to go away for another year's course but I could see it would be valuable in the long term, and so I applied to Barnardo's for secondment.

During the summer, I had joined a sailing club on the Isle of Sheppey where they had several Mirror 16s that were able to race together. Graham used to enjoy crewing on this boat and we could take on board a third person who was less experienced. When we went there, we often took a Mirror dinghy on the roof rack, so that two more children could sail. On one occasion, we were taking part in the club's so-called 'long distance race', which was not much longer than an ordinary race but slightly more out to sea than usual. Sam was supposed to be the third crew member, but when it looked as though it was blowing a force four, I suggested to Sam that it might be a little rough going. He replied in a fit of bravado, "The rougher the better." After we had been sailing for half an hour and about a mile off shore, Sam suddenly asked how far we were from land. I told him that it was behind the mainsail and so he could not see it, but I did not point out that it was looking some distance away! I was very careful not to go full speed on this occasion and let the other Mirror 16s go past us. Learning to bring upright a capsized dinghy was an important part of safety training but I was not going to frighten Sam with a capsize drill away from the shore. There were rescue boats in attendance if needed but there were 'times and places'. Once we had come ashore, Sam was full of bravado again but underneath I could see that although he had gained in confidence, the trip had been a lesson to show respect for the power of wind and water.

The sailing club on the Isle of Sheppey put up some wooden chalets in its grounds, which were available on a lease to members. We decided to take one. We would use it on our day off and take three or four from the Oakwood youngsters with us in the holidays. Besides accommodation for Eileen, Anne and myself, we had bunk beds in one bedroom and two convertible settees in the lounge, giving us room for four youngsters. We could stop overnight and give the children an experience of living in smaller numbers as well as having a more one to one relationship with them. Of course, not all the children who came would necessarily be sailors. This became a popular resource for the children as well as giving us an opportunity to relate more closely to them.

Normally, we did not worry much about days off as we saw the work as a way of life rather than a nine to five job. After all, in Oakwood we had most of our meals with the staff and children seven days a week. One girl one day said to me, "You are lucky that you do not have to go to work. You just play games with us." I think that she thought that when the children were at school the staff went to bed! We had a policy of not making the children think that we were doing a job involving being on and off duty, but we were looking after them like any family, although rather a large one. The staff would say they were going shopping or having a rest and they would attend to the child's request when they came back. They did not say that they could not help because they were going off duty. Working in Barnardo's, we were able to give a continuity of care, which could not be done working a limited number of hours a week on a timetable. Once all the staff in all children's homes were working a fixed number of hours a week, the standard of residential care could never be as good.

By October, we had all the boats safely stored in the boathouse, as we rather grandly referred to the shed. We had the usual Halloween parties in the three houses and Christmas was not far away. We no longer had the Round Table giving us a firework display as we were too near other houses for a big bonfire. The staff made their own arrangements to attend one of the public displays in the city. The one run by the Scouts was a particularly popular one.

Christmas crept up on us once again. We felt a lot had happened since our first Christmas at Woodlands when the fire alarm went off on Christmas Eve. Pinewood and Cedarwood now planned their own Christmas celebrations, but we shared in some activities, such as parties, in the games room. My school friend Matt continued to visit us, especially at Christmas, Easter and bank holidays. Christmas 1968 was memorable for a craze in Oakwood for playing Mah Jong. Matt spent most of his time playing Mah Jong with the youngsters. In addition to my set of Mah Jong, Matt had given the group his set, and so we were able to keep eight players occupied over most of that Christmas period.

Among my New Year resolutions, I decided to apply for a place on the course at Bristol, which meant that if I was successful, I would start in September.

In April, we had another wedding when Betty was married and her sisters, Dawn and Milly were bridesmaids as well as two young bridesmaids from the bridegroom's family. The three sisters looked very attractive in their wedding outfits and we took some nice photographs of the occasion. The wedding took place in Maidstone and so we were not responsible for the reception this time.

A Barnardo's home near Oxford organised an annual regatta and invited other Barnardo's homes to join them on one Saturday in June. We thought we were sufficiently competent now to give it a go. The races would be sailed in a gravel pit, which was normally used by a local sailing club, and they would assist with the organisation. Our sailors were very keen to take part, even though I warned them that sailing on inland waters demanded a very different skill to sailing on the sea. I told them they would find it was more of a delicate touch that was required to keep the boat moving when the wind speed dropped. Quite unlike the sort of sailing they were used to, where brute force was often required. It was significant that the races were to be held on one of the longest days in June because it was certainly going to be a long day for us.

Now it was necessary to sort out who would go on this trip. In Oakwood there were fairly constant changes in the residents as some of the youngsters either returned to their homes or left us for work situations and their places were taken up by others. This meant that no sooner had I taught them to be competent sailors, they moved away and I had to start again. However, I do know that some of them were able to enjoy sailing after they had left us. We could manage to take four of the children and three boats to Oxford. Thank goodness for 'police springs'. Jenny had been in Oakwood since we had moved in but Gillian had only come to us the previous year from a local authority near to London. Her report said that she had dreams and nightmares of drowning. I told the social worker that we would be pleased to accept her in Oakwood and, of course, there would be no expectancy of her joining in the sailing. – Gillian would not be the only one who did not wish to go sailing. Gillian spoke with a cockney accent and wore her hair across her face. She took some time to settle in and I was most surprised when one day Gillian asked to do the swimming test, which was a prerequisite before anyone could go out in the boats. She proved to be a most competent swimmer and passed the test. Gillian enjoyed the sailing and quite rapidly settled in. At the end of the summer, when we brought the boats back to Woodlands, she was heard to comment, "I can't half wait for the beginning of the next sailing season."

The two skippers would be the more experienced boys, Graham and Terry. We discussed with the crews which boats to take and in the end decided to take the Enterprise, which was most suited to inland sailing but could be too likely to capsize in strong winds unless it had a hefty crew. We would also take the two Mirror dinghies. We planned to tow the Enterprise with a Mirror upside down on top of the Enterprise and we would pack all our sailing gear into the Enterprise. The other Mirror would go upside down on the roof rack and the mast of the Enterprise, some 18ft long, would be lashed to the roof rack.

We loaded up everything the night before and went to bed early because we planned to leave about 6am in order to be ready for the first race at 11am. We got off punctually with Eileen navigating in the front seat and four rather sleepy but excited girls and boys in the back seat. All went well and Eileen got us to the right gravel pit but the approach to the gravel pit was down a rather bumpy unmade lane. Unfortunately, on a particularly nasty bump, the Enterprise jumped sideways on the trailer out of one of the supporting brackets and landed on the wrong part of the support, which pierced the hull leaving a hole about 2x3in. Fortunately, I had brought with me a glass fibre repair kit, which enabled me to complete a temporary repair and seal up the hole and the boat was ready for sailing in no time. The youngsters were very relieved to see we had the three boats in working order. They really thought the Enterprise was out of action for the day.

Our crews began to get used to the waters by the end of the day and managed not to capsize. There was a staff race where an adult had to crew and one of the girls or boys took the helm. One of the members of the sailing club went with Terry in the Enterprise and I crewed for Graham in one of our Mirrors. After a couple of races, we were given refreshments before completing the afternoon races. We then had the prize giving and I was pleased to note that each member of our group had won at least one prize. They certainly had not disgraced themselves.

After more refreshments, we packed up our boats and left the sailing club about 7pm and began the long journey home. Eileen had to keep awake as she was navigating, but those in the back seat were soon asleep. It had been a good day all round and a great experience for the children, who enjoyed it so much more when they were in a small group. On the way home, I had to stop two or three times for a break as I was feeling very tired after a long day. We eventually got back after ten o'clock.

I had an invitation to attend an interview at Bristol for the advanced course starting in October 1969. The interview went quite well, I thought, and I very much felt it was the right thing for me to do and I hoped that I would get accepted. It was no good making plans until I knew if I would be going to Bristol, but there was a lot to think about.

Fred was a 15-year-old boy who had been with us at Chilton Park and had had one leg amputated prior to admission, and he now moved into Oakwood from Pinewood. As he would soon be leaving school, it was thought that he should be with boys of his own age. I had already made a relationship with him, occasionally taking him to wrestling matches, and so I was sure he would settle in well, although he had many problems.

One day I had a telephone call from a restaurant in Canterbury where I had placed Richard as an apprentice chef some three years before. The proprietor said that he had to sack Richard because he insisted on putting his own ingredients into sauces when he was told to make a traditional sauce. He said that on many occasions customers had complimented him on his cooking but every now and again he would do his own thing and customers would complain. This had happened once too often and the restaurant would be losing customers. Richard did not appear to be too upset and promptly applied to the Army Catering Corps. Unfortunately, Richard was slap-dash with his educational test paper and he failed the Catering Corps standard, and was offered the job of a soldier in the infantry. He retook the test and passed the Catering Corps standard this time.

The southern area Mirror dinghy championships were being held over a weekend at Hastings in Kent, not so far away. We decided to enter two Mirrors for the event and as Barnardo's had a home in Hastings, we got agreement to pitch our two tents in the grounds. Graham and Jenny wanted to come with us and also Sam. However, I told Sam I didn't feel he really showed very much interest in sailing as he was always 'missing' when it was time to prepare the boats or put them away. He implored me to allow him to come with us, as we were camping at his previous Barnardo's home. I relented and agreed he that could come, but I told him the crew had already been picked.

It was now the summer holidays and we were able to depart at leisure on the Friday afternoon. We had an easy journey and on arrival, Eileen and I introduced ourselves to the head of the home, who showed us where we could camp. That evening, we had time for a quick look at the sea where we would be sailing, and hoped that conditions would be as good tomorrow. We got up in good time on Saturday morning and we were pleased that the weather forecast was still sounding good. Graham and Jenny enjoyed their sail without being spectacular, and Anne and I only achieved a full page colour picture in a yachting magazine, advertising Mirror dinghies! I was not aware of the picture being taken until some time later when I came across it in the magazine. I suppose we made a colourful picture with a yellow and white spinnaker, a yellow painted boat and our royal blue and red anoraks. Sam distinguished himself by helping to launch or recover practically every Mirror dinghy. I think he got the message that it was not always the smart thing to do, to avoid work! This was quite a turning point for him and he very much enjoyed his sailing after this.

During the summer, I heard that I had been accepted for the Bristol course, which would start in October. Eileen had been anxious that there would be sufficient boys and girls capable of acting as skipper or crew in our boats while I was away at Bristol. I decided to run a crash course over three or four days, depending on the weather, based in our chalet on the Isle of Sheppey. Almost next to our chalet was a small stretch of water, the end of a small canal, which would make an ideal sail training course.

We invited Sam, Penny, Graham and Rickey. Penny and Rickey had recently moved into Oakwood and were keen to learn to sail. Eileen needed to be back at Oakwood and Helen, a student doing her practical placement, was chosen to join us. I took the two Mirror dinghies and some empty plastic bottles. I was going to tie a weight to the bottles and use them as marker buoys for our practice sailing in the canal.

The first two days were very basic instruction on safety, rigging the boats and basic sailing round the course, which I had set with the aid of the marker buoys. Then, with Sam and Graham acting as skippers, we got down to some serious competition between the two boats. Each 'race' was quite short owing to the limitations of the canal, but it was the exercise of starting, changing the angle of the sails, rounding the buoys and avoiding collisions that I wanted them to experience. They got plenty of chances to experience these in the confined waters. I wanted them to find out things for themselves and to be able to learn from their mistakes.

Often the race would start with the crew having to rig the boat, launch it and then complete so many laps. As the water was only 3ft deep, it did not matter when things went wrong. They learnt by their mistakes how to rig the boat correctly and on one occasion Sam realised how much faster the boat would go if he raised the rudder slightly when sailing with wind behind him. In trying to beat the other boat, he raised it too high and it came completely out of the water. However, he did not realise what he had done, and without being able to steer the boat, he went straight into the bank, which at the point of collision consisted of a lump of concrete. The boat was soon temporarily repaired with fibre glass and sailing resumed. After three intensive days, we returned to Oakwood having completed our task.

When we joined the local table tennis league, we found it was hard for the younger players to get league experience because late nights made it impossible for them to complete their homework. I made a suggestion to the committee of the Canterbury league, of which I was a member, that Eileen and I would run a Saturday afternoon league for the younger players. I suggested that we used the hall that the league used. This hall had space for six tables and the committee agreed to hire it for six Saturdays and see how well it was supported.

We circulated the information that we would be starting a league to all youth organisations in the area. Our youngsters wanted to join and we felt it was better for them to get out and meet fresh people. Actually, we were pleased they came along as only a very few boys and girls came along to the first three Saturdays. We let them play each other and I gave them a little coaching. By the fourth Saturday, we had enough to start the league and we asked youngsters to split up in pairs and give themselves a team name. We said that each team would play two singles and a doubles against each other in each match.

By word of mouth the news soon got round and we found we no longer had any vacancies. I was off to Bristol in October and Eileen said she could manage to carry on running the junior table tennis league by herself. We were very fortunate that Eileen carried on as the junior league continued to expand to having two sessions on Saturday afternoons. Subsequently, the junior league flourished and others took over the running of the league. As the boys and girls grew too old for the league, they were able to join the senior league with the advantage of several years' experience.

It was very soon time for me to pack my bags and head for Bristol, leaving Eileen once again to take charge on her own.

Chapter 27

Training and then Back to Sailing

I had already thought that I would need my car at Bristol so I drove there on a fine autumn day, wondering what lay in store or me. First of all, I missed my family and then I missed being part of a community. All of a sudden, I felt quite lonely. I knew that once I had met my fellow students and started on the course, things would feel different.

I had decided when I accepted a place on the Bristol course that I would come home for each weekend, when possible. We knew of several married couples whose marriages had suffered as a result of attending a similar course. In such cases, it was not clear whether the separation had already started before the course commenced and attending the course gave them a breather, or whether it was a result of the course itself. Our marriage was precious to us and we felt it was important for each other and Anne that we preserved the continuity. Also, it was important for the children that I was still around and they did not suffer from another break in their lives. There rarely is the right time to move away from children in your care.

On Friday, I would catch the train to London immediately after our afternoon lecture and arrive at Canterbury station in the early evening. Eileen would usually meet me at the station and we would go straight away to have a Chinese meal and catch up on each other's news. On Saturday, I would be involved with Anne and the children and then a quiet evening with Eileen.. This gave us as chance to discuss any problems Eileen was having at Woodlands. Sundays went by very quickly. After attending church in the morning, by four o'clock I found myself with Eileen, and sometimes Anne, on the station platform, saying goodbye. I think there is nothing so dreary and depressing as a railway station on a Sunday. My return home each weekend was working out very well and I found I could catch up with my reading and writing on the train journeys.

Eileen and I had been discussing the idea of her doing the Bristol course when I had completed my course. She had obtained an agreement in principle that Barnardo's would support her application and we felt that with the future of Woodlands uncertain, another string to her bow would be a wise move. I spoke to my tutor about Eileen's application and he was delighted with the thought that we would be his first married couple to do the course, but added that obviously she would have to earn her place in her own right. I brought a set of application papers home as a Christmas present for Eileen!

I was looking forward to having a week at home at Christmas before going to Sheffield for my practical placement. When I arrived at Woodlands, I found half the staff were down with 'flu. I waded in and was happy to be with the children and staff again. After a few days, I succumbed to the epidemic but stayed on my feet until after my Christmas dinner. It was our custom to take the staff out to a Chinese dinner over the Christmas holiday. This year, Eileen played hostess and took the staff out to the meal whilst I got out of bed and into my dressing gown and looked after the Oakwood children in the lounge. We played a new board game called the Business Game. Every time the game got exciting, I came out in a hot sweat! As a result of my bout of sickness, I had to delay my trip to Sheffield for a few days.

Eileen had a very good idea. It was to invite social workers involved with the children of Woodlands to an evening meal in Oakwood, with as many of our staff as were available. The Oakwood children readily agreed to help prepare the meal and serve at the table. It was a great success as it gave an opportunity for residential workers and social workers to get to know one another. The Oakwood youngsters not only got to know their social workers in a less formal setting, but enjoyed dining on the leftovers. It was decided to repeat the event on an annual basis.

In the spring of 1970, Steve, one of our boys who was with us at Chilton Park, was married to a local girl and Anne was invited to be one of two bridesmaids. Anne was now 15 years old and looked very grown up in her long bridesmaid dress. I was again sorry I had to miss this wedding.

Also that spring, we had the first christening that was celebrated in Woodlands. Maria and her husband had their daughter christened and afterwards everyone went back to Oakwood. It was quite a reunion as Milly and Betty and their husbands and Fred and his wife were all present. It must have been a lovely day for all, and I was again sorry to miss this occasion.

The local members of the Round Table continued to give us support and one day we were talking of things they could do to help. We happened to mention how children in care often had very little experience of normal family life. We endeavoured to fill some of these omissions as much as we could with individual or small group outings, but the cost had to come out of our pockets and had to be limited. The Round Table members offered to invite our older children, two or three at a time, to an evening out with their own families. We were delighted with this suggestion as we felt it was just what was needed. These outings were greatly enjoyed by the youngsters, who frequently recounted their various experiences. These outings helped them to gain confidence in social behaviour as well as widening their experience of being in a small group.

While I was away on my placement during the Easter holidays, Eileen had been invited to Bristol for an interview, following her application for a place on the next year's course. It was unfortunate that I was not at Bristol at that time, so we missed seeing each other. After a few weeks of anxious waiting, Eileen received a letter confirming that she had been offered a place on the Bristol course and would be seconded by Barnardo's. I was sorry that we would be parted once again, but in the long run it would be to our advantage

– and anyway, she deserved to go after keeping things running whilst I was away for two courses.

Alongside making plans for the children, we had to consider our own situation. We spoke to Barnardo's about our future and they told us they would like us to run an intermediate treatment centre in South London. Intermediate treatment was the latest idea in childcare. The aim was to provide an opportunity for children at risk or who had committed offences to partake in various activities and form relationships which hopefully would help them to get away from the problems they were experiencing and find more positive activities. Barnardo's were planning to establish such a centre, which would provide for both residential and non-resident youngsters. However, plans had not been drawn up yet, but a site was available. The South London area office wanted both of us to attend periodic meetings so that plans could be made and the situation reviewed.

After another term at Bristol and successfully completing the course, I returned full of energy and glad to get back to Woodlands. The inhabitants of Oakwood had changed considerably whilst I had been away. We now had four boys (the room for visiting old boys now being used for the fourth boy), namely Ricky, Sam, Desmond and Fred. The girls were now April, June and Penny. Desmond had moved in from Pinewood and June (sister of Terry and Philip) had moved over from Cedarwood. Philip and his brother Terry were now both at work, and had been running one of the sailing club's rescue boats during the summer. This was a most responsible job and they had been asked to run the rescue boat, among others, at a regatta week, at one of the sailing clubs on the Isle of Sheppey. I had acquired a Fireball dinghy, which the children and I were very keen to get on the water. The Fireball is a fast racing dinghy just over 16ft long, and the crew helped to balance the boat on a trapeze attached to a harness worn by the crew. It was quite safe for the crew but more exciting and required a degree of skill, especially when using a spinnaker. There were already two of these boats racing in the club.

Fred had by now left school and had a job in a department store, but I am afraid things were not going too well for him. We tried to give him every support. The children now knew of the closure of Woodlands and arrangements were being discussed with the appropriate social workers, children and our staff for the most suitable placements for them, and the timescale involved. We expected Woodlands to be open for at least another year and quite a number of the older children would have moved on naturally by that time. A lot of time and effort was going into making the movements of the children as positive as we could with the minimum of disturbance to them.

While I had been away at Bristol, Eileen had done a good job to keep the sailing going for the children with all her other extra tasks. As I had now returned from the course, there was some expectation from Ricky, Sam, June and Penny that they would get some more sailing before the summer ended. There was a sailing club near Poole in Dorset, which organised an annual regatta that lasted for a week. They had a separate class for racing Fireballs and the secretary told me that they would welcome any spare crew I brought with me, as there was always a demand for a spare crew. This would save me bringing anther boat. We managed to book a six-berth caravan for the week. Unfortunately, Eileen was busy getting ready to leave Woodlands for her course and could not come and so I asked Veronica to come. Veronica was a student on a practical placement and it would give her some valuable experience.

After a safe journey, delayed by a vicious thunderstorm that filled my boat with rainwater, we found our campsite. Next morning, we went down to the sailing club and announced our arrival. Ricky was offered the chance to crew in a big boat and Sam was offered a place in an Enterprise. That left Penny to crew the Fireball with me. They were all looking forward to the first race next day.

The weather was fine but lacked much wind, and Sam did very well and was especially valued for his light weight. His Enterprise had very good results and the owner was well pleased. Ricky seemed to spend most of the time below deck preparing spinnakers for hoisting, the idea being that the spinnaker was packed in a roll and tied with very thin string which broke once the sail was hoisted and prevented the sail getting tangled up. However, I think he was quite proud of being a member of the crew in a big boat and would carry those memories for many a year. Penny and I had a pleasant but not too exciting week. We took one day off sailing and visited local places of interest including the famous Poole Pottery where I bought a small present for Eileen. We all returned home safely and I felt the young people had some satisfactory sailing and happy memories. Veronica had done very well looking after us all and keeping us well fed. I think she rather enjoyed a change from routine.

Rickey and I entered the Fireball in the Medway regatta, a weekend event, taking place at Rochester on the Medway. River sailing was a challenge to us, and we were looking forward to sailing in races in the Fireball group and not a mixed group where we would all race on different handicaps. On the first day, we found that we were racing in a group of 17 Fireballs and we didn't expect to do very well with our lack of experience. However, we managed some good starts and on one occasion, we were first for the first few hundred yards, only to be overtaken by half the fleet by the end of that race.

On the second race the next day, the last race of the regatta, we were sailing in very light winds and were last by a long way, struggling against tide and wind. As we came round the final bend before the finish line, we could see the rest of the Fireballs just a few hundred yards from the finish-line, not making any progress, only just able to hold their position against the tide due to the failing wind. They were all bunched on the left-hand side of the river close to the bank where the adverse tide was not so strong. I suggested to Rickey that as we had nothing to lose, I was going to take a gamble and creep up towards the finish line, hugging the right-hand bank. This tactic involved crossing the river and in the centre, the adverse current would be much stronger. As we found ourselves near the centre of the river, the boat was pushed back quite quickly. Rickey kept saying we should go back to our previous side, but I said we had lost too much ground already crossing the river, and were committed. To our delight, over the next 20 minutes or so, we gradually crept along the right-hand bank and caught up the Fireball fleet who were stemming the tide but were not making any forward progress. Then, to our amazement, we continued to make almost imperceptible progress to the finish line and won the race!

Rickey soon forgot his complaints as we walked into an empty changing room and realised we were not only the first Fireball to finish, but the first boat in the regatta to finish. It was rather amusing when we went back to our Fireball to see a small crowd of people, presumably Fireball sailors, carefully studying our boat. It appeared that they were trying to see what we had that they did not have on their boat. The answer was simple – luck! It did not stop us enjoying our victory.

Chapter 28

Farewell Barnardo's

Darker evenings and cooler nights signalled the end of summer. The children went back to school and Eileen began to get ready for the Bristol course. We had made good progress with the social workers, planning for the placements of the children, which took priority for the next 12 months. Our own future plans were more uncertain. We wanted to remain working for Barnardo's and they had offered us the joint post to run the intermediate treatment centre in London, but it was only in the planning stage. They had offered Eileen the temporary position of matron in charge of an adolescent girls' home and suggested I could have the job of social worker, until the unit was built. Unfortunately, Barnardo's could not guarantee that we would be living in the one locality for the next two years after Woodlands closed. In a year's time, Anne would be starting her 'A' level course and we wanted to avoid a change of schools in the middle of her course. Our alternative was to see what happened to Woodlands.

With her mother at Bristol during the week, we had agreed that I had breakfast with Anne in the spare bedroom in our flat upstairs. This would enable me to give Anne my undivided attention at least once a day. This worked out very well and we both enjoyed this time together.

Mealtimes, especially teatimes, tended to become a prolonged affair when all sorts of topics were discussed, often at some length. I don't think it was just a case of putting off the washing-up! Anne used to be a bit frustrated when it was her turn to wash up as she liked to get it all over quickly as she was now going to the technical school and had a lot of homework.

One mealtime, the subject of staff meetings came up. I was asked why we had them and if the children could be represented by some of the older ones. The debate continued over several days and after discussion with the staff, we agreed that we would have weekly meetings with the Oakwood youngsters. I said to them that they could have a form of self-government. We would have a weekly meeting of staff and residents when any suggestion or ideas for the improvement of life in Oakwood, or complaints, could be raised. I reserved the right not to follow up anything if I felt it not to be in their best interests. We would continue to have these weekly meetings as long as we had over half of the youngsters attending.

The meetings went very well with everyone attending. One rule we had always had was that between 6pm and 7pm the children went to their rooms and completed their homework. If they did not have homework to do, they still had to go to their bedroom and could engage in any quiet activity. This gave those with homework the opportunity to complete it without being sidetracked by those who did not have any. Sam brought up this subject because he was coming home late from school, as he was taking part in rehearsals for the school play. After he had eaten his tea, one of the house-mothers had ruled that he still had to have a quiet hour in his room irrespective of how much homework he had to do. Sam complained to me and I told him to bring it up at the next weekly meeting. Much to Sam's distress, all the other children voted that he should complete his hour of quiet time in his room. I thought this was a little harsh on him and we brought up a compromise at a future meeting.

A more positive decision was a request to have a Chinese meal on a Saturday teatime. I agreed to subsidise it but would want a fixed contribution from each of the children. Sam was the only one against having a Chinese meal and chose fish and chips. Edna and Pam agreed to cook some fried egg rice and to warm the plates while I went out to buy the food. On my return with the food and something to drink, I found everything ready and the rice cooked. Everyone enjoyed their meal except Rickey who demanded his money back. I told him that he was extremely fortunate to find out that he did not like Chinese food at a cost of a few pence rather than having to spend several pounds on a meal out. After all, he could have chosen fish and chips. The children learnt a lot from these meetings and I wished that I had introduced them earlier in Oakwood.

Fred had lost his job at the big store in Canterbury and we found a job that seemed more suitable. It was a small factory near the railway station in Dover, which made electrical components. Fred's job would be to help assemble electrical plugs. This would involve screwing in the small screws in the terminals that gripped the wires in place. Fred could go from Canterbury by train as it was only a short walk to the factory and coming back, he could get a bus from Canterbury station to a bus stop near Woodlands. The only snag was that he would have to catch a train to Dover at 7am. As there was not a convenient bus at that time, I would have to be up early and give Fred a lift to the station. I thought this was well worth it in order to get Fred into a job.

All went well until one day I received a telephone call from Fred's boss who complained that Fred was cross-threading the screws when he was screwing them into the plug. He agreed that Fred could bring home the faulty ones and correct them in the evening each day. Unfortunately, Fred brought home so many faulty plugs that he could not mend them all by himself. We used to all help out and worked like a production unit, spread round the dining table. I think it would have been easier if I went to Dover and did Fred's job for him! I suppose it was worth it even though it only kept him in work for a few more months.

Eileen came back from Bristol for Christmas and although enjoying the course, like me was rather anxious about our future plans and its significance for Anne. We decided to approach Kent County Council, as it appeared that they were going to lease the building from Barnardo's when Woodlands closed. We had an interview with officers of the Children's Department of Kent County

Council in June, and were offered the post of superintendent and matron of Woodlands with the option of running an establishment for adolescent girls with problems or an assessment and reception centre, both of which were urgently needed by the county. We decided, after much thought, to go for the assessment centre. Eileen asked her tutor on the Bristol course for her final placement to be in an assessment centre to give her additional experience. Barnardo's agreed that this was the best option for us as they could not promise that we could be in one place for two years while Anne completed her 'A' levels.

Eileen successfully finished the course at Bristol and came home, pleased to be united with her family again. Just to complete the circle, we had one more wedding to attend. Our other Fred, who was one of the original boys in the Barkingside cottage 12 years before, was married in London and Anne was a bridesmaid. This was a very happy occasion.

It had been a very busy year with all the arrangements that had to be made because of the closure of Woodlands, scheduled for 31st July, and the takeover by Kent County Council of the buildings, including Eileen and me, on 1st August. Apart from the priority of trying to make sure that the most suitable placements were found for the children that were affected by this event, many of the staff had been forced to seek other positions and there was a rather heavy atmosphere during the last few months. There had not been a lot of time for sailing and other activities, although we did try to keep life as positive as possible for those still at Woodlands.

It was decided to have a 'farewell' social gathering and invite any children and staff who had previously been with us at Woodlands or Chilton Park and also social workers and Barnardo's staff with whom we had worked. The Saturday we chose turned out to be a lovely sunny day and gave people the chance to say their own farewells to each other or plan future contacts.

We had enjoyed 12 years caring for the children within the Barnardo's family and would miss the daily contact with them. The children knew where we were and we said we would always be pleased to see or hear from them in the future, if they wished to keep in contact with us.

Chapter 29

And so to the Future – a Brief Summary

Now began a new chapter in our childcare work, which turned out to have plenty of variety. For the next year, Eileen and I worked together to set up the assessment centre for Kent County Council. Teachers had to be appointed and an educational unit established on the premises, as well as appointing staff for the physical and social care of the children. Many of the children that came to us came through the courts, but all of those admitted would only be at the centre for a few months. During this time, an assessment had to be made as to which was the best placement to meet their needs. We worked very closely with the social workers, psychologists, teachers and childcare staff, as well as listening to the children themselves. After a year, Eileen left to work as a tutor on a childcare course at Maidstone Technical College whilst I remained at Woodlands in charge of the unit. As time went on, we decided that although we found our present work very worthwhile, we did not see this as our long-term future.

In the summer of 1972, Anne successfully completed her 'A' level exams and was on her way to university, which allowed us the freedom to consider our plans. We started looking at advertisements to see what opportunities were open to us. We saw one advertisement which interested us and sent for details. It was for a superintendent and matron at a home for 60 children in Jersey. The home included a nursery unit, a long-stay unit and was the only resource on the island for placing children committed by the courts. We went for an interview and were amazed at the place. I told the officer who was showing us round that it was 30 years behind the times! He agreed and said a change was wanted. He said that the plan would be that we would work for three months and then put in a report on what needed to be done. Eileen and I talked long and hard about accepting these posts, but we saw it as a challenge as there was obviously a lot of work to be done there.

In June 1972, I started work as superintendent of Haut de la Garenne. Eileen came over to Jersey each weekend and joined me permanently in the September, when the course on which she tutored had ended. We soon realised the extent of the changes needed. We also quickly found how any changes we wanted to make were strongly opposed by the staff of the home and made very difficult. The home was very under-staffed and it was obvious that we were very much resented by the staff. We felt the first step to make any progress was the appointment of more staff who would work with us and this was one of the main points I made in my report on recommendations for improvement. The result of my report was minimal. There was not much money but the committee would give us ONE extra member of staff. We felt extremely deflated by this and decided that with the staff against us and no real support from the children's committee, we were in a no-win situation, and we handed in our notices, although we had no jobs to go to. As it happened, we were due to have a week's leave starting the next day, when we were flying back to England. That afternoon, we had a visit from the director of education and the chairman of the children's committee, and we were asked to reconsider our decision. We were told the committee would not accept our notices until our return, so that we had time to think things over. On our return, we told the committee that we had both been offered work and we would be leaving after we had worked out our three months' notice.

In February 1973, we returned to England, bitterly disappointed that we had not been able to do much to improve the situation at the children's home. During our eight months on the island, we were completely unaware of any abuse of children, either then or previous to our appointments.

On our visit to England in November, I had been offered the post of children's homes adviser with the London Borough of Brent, and Eileen the post of training officer with the National Children's Homes, subject to references. I spent a very positive time in Brent in the Social Services Department and in 1975 I applied for the post of principal officer responsible for residential childcare in the Social Services Department of the Royal Borough of Kensington and Chelsea, where I worked happily until I retired.

Eileen's career was interrupted by the ill health of my elderly parents who needed to come and live with us, and consequently she wished to work nearer home. Eileen worked mainly with the London Borough of Redbridge as principal officer in charge of provision for children. However, for the last five years of her working life with Redbridge, she enjoyed a challenge by accepting the post of principal officer for the elderly within the borough, a position she found very stimulating and rewarding.

As we look back over our time in childcare, we have no regrets about our decision in 1959 to give up our police and teaching careers to work for Barnardo's. We get great joy from seeing so many of the children we cared for now living happy and settled lives, particularly that the families of brothers and sisters are still very much in touch with each other.

We saw great changes in childcare policy over the years and were particularly affected by the decision by the Barnardo's Council in 1969 to change the emphasis of their work with the advances of state welfare, which involved the closure of most traditional children's homes, including Woodlands. We have great admiration for the way Barnardo's have moved with the times to meet the current needs of children.